WORLD IN FOCUS

FOCUS ON
ISRAEL

ALEX WOOLF

WORLD ALMANAC® LIBRARY

Please visit our web site at: www.garethstevens.com
For a free color catalog describing World Almanac® Library's list of high-quality books
and multimedia programs, call 1-800-848-2928 (USA) or 1-800-387-3178 (Canada).
World Almanac® Library's fax: (414) 332-3567.

Library of Congress Cataloging-in-Publication Data

Woolf, Alex.
     Focus on Israel / Alex Woolf. — North American ed.
       p. cm. — (World in focus)
     Includes bibliographical references and index.
     ISBN-13: 978-0-8368-6735-0 (lib. bdg.)
     ISBN-13: 978-0-8368-6742-8 (softcover)
     1. Israel—Juvenile literature. I. Title.
     DS102.95.W66   2007
     956.94—dc22   2006027641

This North American edition first published in 2007 by
World Almanac® Library
A Member of the WRC Media Family of Companies
330 West Olive Street, Suite 100
Milwaukee, WI 53212 USA

This U.S. edition copyright © 2007 by World Almanac® Library. Original edition
copyright © 2007 by Wayland. First published in 2007 by Wayland, an imprint
of Hachette Children's Books, 338 Euston Road, London NW1 3BH, U.K.

Commissioning editor: Nicola Edwards
Editor: Nicola Barber
Inside design: Chris Halls, www.mindseyedesign.co.uk
Cover design: Wayland
Series concept and project management by EASI-Educational Resourcing
(info@easi-er.co.uk)
Statistical research: Anna Bowden
Maps and graphs: Martin Darlison, Encompass Graphics

World Almanac® Library editor: Alan Wachtel
World Almanac® Library cover design: Scott Krall

Picture acknowledgements. The author and publisher would like to thank the following for allowing their pictures to be reproduced
in this publication:
CORBIS cover (top), 28, 29 (Paul A. Souders), cover (bottom), title page, 14, 16, 21, 26, 27, 50, 53, 57 (Richard T. Nowitz),
4 (Patrick Robert/Sygma), 5, 15 (Hanan Isachar), 6 (Benjamin Rondel), 8 (Nathan Benn), 9, 49 (Gil Cohen Magen/Reuters),
10, 11 (Bettmann), 12 (Reuters), 13 (Mahfouz Abu Turk/Reuters), 17, 25 (Ricki Rosen), 18, 19, 43 (Annie Griffiths Belt),
20 (Barbara Davidson/Dallas Morning News), 22 (Dave Bartruff), 23, 55 (David Rubinger), 24 (Kevin Frayer-Pool/epa),
30 (Eldad Rafaeli), 31 (Nik Wheeler), 32 (Attal Serge/Sygma), 33 (Morton Beebe), 34, 42 (Gyori Antoine/Sygma),
35 (Gil Cohen Magen/RNPS/Reuters), 36 (Reuters), 37 (Chip East/Reuters), 38 (James Marshall), 39 (Ed Kashi), 40 (Koren Ziv/Sygma),
41 (Kontos Yannis/Sygma), 44 (Ammar Awad/Reuters), 45 (Yossi Zamir/Pool/Reuters), 46 (David H. Wells), 47 (Gleb Garanich/Reuters),
51 (Goran Topmasevic/Reuters), 52 (Jim Hollander/epa), 54 (Alberto Denkberg/Reuters), 56 (Steve Kaufman), 58 (Damir Sagolj/Reuters),
59 (Yonathan Weitzman); Easi-Images 48 (Roy Maconachie).

The directional arrow portrayed on the map on page 7 provides only an approximation of north.
The data used to produce the graphics and data panels in this title were the latest available at the time of production.
Wherever possible, the data used in this book refers specifically to Israel as specified by the relevant source documents.
However, some data sets (where their composition is not clarified) may incorporate data relating to the Palestinian Territories.

Printed in China

1 2 3 4 5 6 7 8 9 10 09 08 07 06

CONTENTS

1 Israel – An Overview   4

2 History   8

3 Landscape and Climate   14

4 Population and Settlements   18

5 Government and Politics   22

6 Energy and Resources   26

7 Economy and Income   30

8 Global Connections   34

9 Transportation and Communications   38

10 Education and Health   42

11 Culture and Religion   46

12 Leisure and Tourism   50

13 Environment and Conservation   54

14 Future Challenges   58

Time Line   60

Glossary   61

Further Information   62

Index   63

About the Author   64

Cover: A view of Jerusalem that shows the Dome of the Rock, the Al-Aqsa Mosque, and the Western Wall of Solomon's Temple.

Title page: Timna Park, in the Negev Desert, is known for its spectacular rock formations.

CHAPTER 1

Israel – An Overview

Israel is a nation in southwestern Asia that is located on a narrow strip of land on the eastern coast of the Mediterranean Sea. It was founded in 1948 as a Jewish state—a country that would serve as the homeland of the Jewish people. Today, four-fifths of its population is Jewish. Many Jews regard Israel as their spiritual home, even if they don't live there, because it was the birthplace of their religion and culture. Almost all non-Jewish Israelis are Palestinian Arabs, and most of them are Muslims.

▼ Israeli soldiers confront Palestinians during the first intifada, which lasted from 1987 to 1993, in the West Bank.

A NATION IN CONFLICT

The current conflict between Israel and the Palestinian Arabs has its roots long before Israel came into existence. To a great extent, it is a dispute about land and who controls it. But mixed in with this is a religious clash between Jews and Muslim Arabs. Some Jews base their claim to the land partly on their belief that it was promised to them by God, as stated in the Bible, and partly on the historic fact that the land was the site of the Jewish kingdoms of Israel and Judah during the first millennium B.C. Probably a larger group of Jews claim that Israel has the right to exist based on the fact that, in 1947, the United Nations (UN)

partitioned the land in question into two states, one Jewish, the other Arab. The Palestinian claim lies in the fact that their people have lived on this land for many hundreds of years. The conflict has been marked by violence and several wars. In recent years there has been some progress toward peace, but attacks on Israel's soldiers in mid 2006 set off the worst fighting in the conflict in decades.

WHERE THREE CONTINENTS MEET

It is understandable that when outside observers think about Israel they focus on the conflict that frequently dominates newspaper headlines around the world, but the country is fascinating for many other reasons. It is located in a place where three continents meet—Africa, Asia, and Europe—and its landscape is a diverse mixture of these three continents, with sandy coastlines,

fertile valleys, mountains, lakes, and deserts. Israel's culture also reflects this fusion of different continents. Its various communities have carried their customs and traditions from many places, including eastern Europe, Russia, the Middle East, and North Africa. Israeli music, for example, mixes eastern and western rhythms.

? Did You Know?

Since its establishment, Israel has encouraged Jews from around the world to settle in the country. By 2006, nearly 2.75 million Jews had emigrated to Israel, more than three times the country's population in 1948.

▼ Israel is a country of diverse and spectacular landscapes, from the imposing cliffs of Mount Arbel, in northern Israel, to the Sea of Galilee (Lake Kinneret), which is visible on the left.

▲ This view of Jerusalem shows the Dome of the Rock and the Al-Aqsa Mosque, along with the Western Wall of Solomon's Temple (lower right).

ANCIENT AND MODERN

Israel's territory is rich in ancient history. It has been fought over and dominated by successive cultures that have each left their distinctive mark on it. Israel is a holy land for three of the world's major religions: Judaism, Christianity, and Islam. Some place names in Israel—Jerusalem, Nazareth, Galilee, the Jordan River—have powerful significance for Jews, Christians, and Muslims alike. Jerusalem, in particular, is full of sites of religious and historic significance, including the remains of Solomon's Temple, the Al-Aqsa Mosque, and the Via Dolorosa.

Israel is also a young, modern, and dynamic nation. The country is one of the world's leading producers of advanced technologies, including electronics and computer software. It also has a highly efficient health care service, a well-developed transportation system, and one of the most up-to-date communications networks in the Middle East.

It is Israel's blend of ancient and modern that makes the country such a unique and fascinating place.

Physical Geography Data

- Land area: 7,847 sq miles/20,330 sq km
- Water area: 170 sq miles/440 sq km
- Total area: 8,017 sq miles/20,770 sq km
- World rank (by area): 154
- Land boundaries: 632 miles/1,017 km
- Border countries: Egypt, Jordan, Lebanon, Syria (plus Gaza Strip and West Bank)
- Coastline: 170 miles/273 km
- Highest point: Har Meron (3,963 ft/1,208 m)
- Lowest point: Dead Sea (-1,339 ft/-408 m)

Source: CIA World Factbook

Legend

★ Capital

● Cities > 200,000

● Cities > 100,000

● Cities > 50,000

• Other cities

▲ Mountain

CHAPTER 2

History

The land now occupied by the modern state of Israel has been the scene of conflict for thousands of years. Many different peoples have invaded and conquered the region.

ISRAEL AND JUDAH

Between 1800 and 1500 B.C., the Hebrew people settled in the region that is modern-day Israel. In around 1000 B.C., King David unified the Hebrew tribes, known by then as Israelites, and formed the kingdom of Israel with its capital in Jerusalem. After the death of King Solomon (David's son) in about 928 B.C., the court in Jerusalem suffered a financial collapse. When it tried to raise taxes, the people in its north refused to pay. As a result, the kingdom split in two: Israel and Judah. From the name Judah came the word *Jew*.

INVASION AND DIASPORA

Israel was wiped out by the Assyrians in the eighth century B.C. Beginning in the sixth century B.C., Judah was conquered by a succession of invaders, including the Babylonians, the Persians, the Greeks, the Romans, and the Byzantines. From about A.D. 70, while under Roman rule, the Jews began to leave Judea (as it had become known by then) and spread all over the world. This migration is known as the Diaspora. By the 700s, Jewish communities had been established as far west as Spain and as far east as China.

The region, by this time known as Palestine, was conquered by Muslim Arabs in the seventh century. It remained under Muslim control until the fall of the Ottoman Empire in 1918, except for a period in the twelfth century when Christian Crusaders ruled Jerusalem.

THE BRITISH MANDATE

In 1917, the British government announced its support for the establishment of a Jewish homeland in Palestine in the Balfour

▶ After the Romans captured Jerusalem in A.D. 70, a small force of about 1,000 Jews held out for two years against the conquerors in the mountain-top fortress of Masada (shown here), located in southeastern Israel.

Declaration, named after British foreign minister Arthur Balfour. Some Arabs believed the Balfour Declaration contradicted what they thought was Britain's earlier promise to Arab nationalist leaders (in 1915–1916) to support an independent Arab state in the same region. In 1920, after the fall of the Ottoman Empire, the League of Nations (an organization of countries set up to promote international peace) placed Palestine under the mandate, or authority, of Britain. Neither Jews nor Arabs were happy to be ruled by Britain, and both peoples desired an independent homeland in Palestine.

Under the British Mandate (1920–1948), clashes between Jewish settlers and Arabs became increasingly violent. Jewish emigration to Palestine increased during the 1930s, particularly when the anti-Semitic Nazi Party came to power in Germany in 1933. After the Holocaust—the systematic extermination of nearly 6 million Jews by the Nazis during World War II—the international community found it harder to ignore Jewish demands for an independent homeland.

► The Hall of Names at the Yad Vashem Holocaust History Museum, is located in Jerusalem. The hall is dedicated to the millions of Jews killed by the Nazis during the Holocaust.

Focus on: The Zionist Movement

During the late nineteenth century, there was a rise in anti-Semitism, or hatred of Jews, in parts of Europe and Russia. Many Jews saw the creation of a Jewish state in Palestine as the best way to protect themselves from anti-Semitism. The Zionist movement was founded with the goal of establishing such a state. Heeding the call of the Zionist movement, large numbers of Jews began to settle in Palestine. Between 1880 and 1914, the Jewish population of Palestine rose from about 15,000 to 60,000, forming about 10 percent of the region's population. Clashes between the new settlers and Palestinian Arabs began in the 1900s.

THE ESTABLISHMENT OF ISRAEL

By 1947, Britain wanted to end its mandate. It was struggling to control the violence between Jews and Palestinian Arabs. The British rulers were also victims of a campaign of bombings and assassinations by Jewish terrorist groups such as the Irgun. They requested help from the United Nations (UN), the successor to the League of Nations. In November 1947, the UN voted to accept a plan to divide Palestine into two states, one Jewish and one Arab. The Jews accepted the plan, but the Arabs rejected it.

Fighting between the two sides broke out immediately. In April 1948, the Irgun massacred a group of Palestinian Arab civilians.

For reasons that are controversial, many Palestinian Arabs fled the conflict, and 726,000 of them became refugees. During the fighting, on May 15, 1948, the British left Palestine, and Jewish leaders declared the founding of the state of Israel. Six neighboring Arab countries (Egypt, Syria, Transjordan, Lebanon, Saudi Arabia, and Iraq) immediately invaded the new state. Despite being outnumbered, Israel's forces were better organized than their opponents and managed to gain territories beyond those they had been allocated by the UN plan.

By the time the war ended in 1949, Israel controlled about 75 percent of Palestine, while neighboring Arab states took over the remaining portions. Transjordan occupied the West Bank, an area west of the Jordan River, and Egypt took over the Gaza Strip, a strip of land on the Mediterranean coast. Both of these areas were to be part of the Palestinian Arab state planned by the UN. The Palestinian Arab state was never founded; none of Israel's Arab neighbors recognized its right to exist; and Israel refused reentry to the refugees, leaving only 150,000 Arabs within its borders. The refugees stayed in the West Bank, the Gaza Strip, and neighboring Arab states.

◄ David Ben-Gurion, Israel's first prime minister, declares the independence of the state of Israel in Tel Aviv on May 14, 1948.

THE SIX-DAY WAR

In June 1967, fearing that it was about to be attacked by its Arab neighbors, Israel launched strikes against Egypt, Jordan (formerly Transjordan), and Syria. In just six days, Israel captured Gaza and the Sinai Peninsula from Egypt; the Golan Heights from Syria; and the West Bank, including East Jerusalem, from Jordan. Israel had more than tripled the territory under its control, and the Jewish state was now in control of more than 750,000 hostile Palestinian Arabs in the West Bank and Gaza Strip (which, together, became known as "the occupied territories"). Many Palestinians now focused their support on the Palestine Liberation Organization (PLO), a coalition of Palestinian groups that began engaging in terrorist actions against Israel.

Focus on: The Suez War

Clashes at the border of Israel and Egypt occurred during the early 1950s. In July 1956, Egyptian leader Gamal Abdel Nasser brought the Suez Canal, which was at that time jointly owned by the British and French, under Egypt's control. (Egypt had previously closed the canal to Israeli shipping and blockaded the Straits of Tiran, another key trading route for Israel.) In response to Nasser's action, Israel, Britain, and France launched a joint attack on Egypt. By November, Israel had captured from Egypt the Gaza Strip and Sinai Peninsula. Under pressure from the UN, however, Israel withdrew to its previous borders in March 1957.

▼ An Israeli army convoy, including a truck containing captured Egyptian soldiers, makes triumphant progress through the Sinai Peninsula during the Six-Day War.

CONFLICTS AND A TREATY

On October 6, 1973—on Yom Kippur, the holiest day of the Jewish calendar—Egypt and Syria invaded Israel. After initial gains, the Arab forces were pushed back by Israel, which reoccupied the Sinai Peninsula. Although Israel won the war, it suffered heavy losses and was shaken by the surprise attack. In 1978, Israel and Egypt negotiated a peace agreement at Camp David, in the United States. The peace treaty was signed in March 1979, and Israel withdrew from the Sinai Peninsula in 1982.

By the mid-1980s, many Palestinians had grown increasingly frustrated at Israel's continuing occupation of the West Bank and Gaza Strip. In 1987, they began the intifada, a mass uprising. Riots took place in many of the towns and cities of the occupied territories. By the time the intifada ended in 1993, over 1,000 Palestinians had been killed.

THE PEACE PROCESS

In the early 1990s, Israel began negotiations with its Arab neighbors and the PLO. One outcome of this was a peace treaty with Jordan in 1994. Talks with the PLO led to the Oslo Accords, signed in 1993. Under the terms of

Focus on: Conflict with Lebanon

In 1982, Israel invaded Lebanon to drive out PLO fighters who had been attacking northern Israel. After a long operation, Israel forced the PLO out, fully withdrawing in 2000. In 2006, Hezbollah fighters attacked Israel from Lebanon, leading to a showdown between Israel and the terrorist group.

▼ Israeli prime minister Yitzhak Rabin (left) shakes hands with Palestinian leader Yasser Arafat at the signing ceremony of the Oslo Accords in September 1993. U.S. president Bill Clinton looks on.

this agreement, Israel agreed to a gradual withdrawal from the occupied territories and the establishment of the Palestinian Authority (PA) as the territories' civil government. Israel, however, retained military control of the area.

By the late 1990s, the peace process had stalled. Radical Islamic groups within the Palestinian community, such as Hamas and Islamic Jihad, opposed any peace with Israel and carried out terrorist attacks against Israel, hardening Israeli attitudes. Israel continued to build Jewish settlements in the occupied territories, further inflaming Arab opinion. Renewed attempts to reach a peace deal in 1998 and 2000 both failed.

THE SECOND INTIFADA AND THE ROAD MAP

A second intifada erupted in September 2000. This time, there was both rioting across the occupied territories and a rise in terrorism, including suicide bombings, inside Israel. In 2002, Israel's forces invaded and reoccupied West Bank towns that had been handed over to the PA in order to destroy the terrorist bases.

In 2003, the UN attempted to restart the peace process by drawing up a "road map to peace." Talks broke down after further terrorist attacks and Israeli military strikes. The two sides made a truce in February 2005. In August, Israel removed all of its settlers and troops from the Gaza Strip and handed the territory over to the PA. In 2006, however, attacks on Israeli soldiers by Hamas and Hezbollah sparked heavy fighting.

? Did You Know?

Since June 2002, Israel has been constructing a "security fence" around the Palestinian-controlled areas of the West Bank as a means of protecting itself against terrorist attacks. In October 2003, the UN passed a resolution saying the fence was "in contradiction to international law." In spite of this, most Israelis are strongly in favor of it.

▼ Part of Israel's security fence that runs through Al-Ram, a suburb of East Jerusalem. Since construction of the wall began, there has been a sharp drop in the number of suicide bombings in Israel.

CHAPTER 3

Landscape and Climate

Israel, based on the frontiers established in 1949, covers an area of about 7,847 square miles (20,330 square kilometers). In 1981, Israel annexed the Golan Heights and East Jerusalem, which together cover a further 173 sq miles (448 sq km), and Israel's government regards these areas as part of its national territory. The UN and most countries, however, do not recognize these annexations. The occupied territory of the West Bank (excluding East Jerusalem) covers 2,262 sq miles (5,860 sq km).

For a small country, Israel has a diverse terrain. It has four major geographical regions: the Mediterranean coastal plain, the Judeo-Galilean Highlands, the Rift Valley, and the Negev Desert.

COASTAL PLAIN AND HIGHLANDS

The Mediterranean coastal plain is a narrow strip of fertile land that borders the Mediterranean from Haifa, in the north, to Gaza in the south. Most of Israel's population, industry, and agriculture is concentrated in this region. In its center is the Plain of Sharon, where most of Israel's citrus crop is grown. The northern part includes part of the fertile and densely populated Plain of Esdraelon.

▼ Timna Park, which is located north of Elat in the Negev Desert, is well known for its spectacular rock formations. The area is also the site of copper mines dating back 6,000 years.

Focus on: The Dead Sea

The Dead Sea lies around 1,339 feet (408 meters) below sea level, making it the lowest natural feature on Earth. It is also the world's saltiest body of water, and it is rich in valuable minerals such as potash, magnesium, bromine, and salt, all of which are mined, mainly for export. The level of the Dead Sea has dropped in recent years, both due to a high rate of evaporation of 5 feet (1.6 m) per year and because the rivers that feed it have been diverted by Israel and Jordan for their water needs, reducing its incoming water by 75 percent. Israel's government is considering a plan to link the Dead Sea with the Mediterranean using a system of pipes and canals. This plan may help to restore the Dead Sea to its original size and level.

◀ The Dead Sea is ten times saltier than the ocean, and no fish can live in it. The high levels of salts and minerals in the sea allow people to float in its waters, which are also said to have health-giving properties.

The Judeo-Galilean Highlands are a series of mountain ranges that run north to south through the center of Israel. The north is dominated by the mountains of Galilee. These include Har (Mount) Meron, which at 3,963 feet (1,208 m) is the highest peak in Israel. South of Galilee are the Judean and Samarian hills, which run through most of the rest of Israel.

RIFT VALLEY AND NEGEV

A long, narrow valley, known as the Rift Valley, runs through eastern Israel, forming part of the Great Rift Valley that extends from Syria to Mozambique. The sides of the Rift Valley are steep, but the floor is mostly flat and much of it lies below sea level. There are few fertile areas in the Rift Valley. The Negev Desert, in the far south, is Israel's driest, most infertile region. It is a triangular-shaped area of flatlands and mountains extending north from the Gulf of Aqaba.

RIVERS, LAKES, AND COASTLINE

The Sea of Galilee (also known as Lake Kinneret) is a large freshwater lake in the northern Rift Valley, covering 64 sq miles (166 sq km). Further south in the Rift Valley is a saltwater lake called the Dead Sea, covering 394 sq miles (1,020 sq km). Both lakes are below sea level.

The Jordan River runs through the northern Rift Valley, flowing through the Sea of Galilee and emptying into the Dead Sea. The two other main rivers of Israel are the Yarkon, which reaches the Mediterranean through Tel Aviv-Yafo, and the Kishon, which runs through Haifa. Israel's coastline, including its western edge bordering the Mediterranean and the southern tip on the Red Sea, stretches for 170 miles (273 km) and is mainly flat and low-lying with few cliffs or headlands.

CLIMATE

Israel has a typical Mediterranean climate, with hot, dry summers and cool, rainy winters. Between May and October, the sun shines almost continuously. A hot, dry, dusty wind called the khamsin sometimes blows from east to west, especially during spring and fall. The hot, dry summers leave much of Israel's landscape parched and brown. But by spring, after the rains of the winter, Israel's countryside can look very green.

TEMPERATURES

Israel's temperatures vary, depending on altitude or exposure to sea breezes. Its hottest month is August, and its coldest month is January. On the Mediterranean coastal plain, which includes Tel Aviv-Yafo and Haifa, August averages 77 °Fahrenheit (25 °Celsius), while January averages 54 °F (12 °C). In upland areas such as Jerusalem, temperatures are cooler. August averages 76 °F (24.5 °C) and January averages 48 °F (9 °C). The hottest areas are at the lowest altitudes. Around the Dead Sea, temperatures can reach 120 °F (49 °C).

RAINFALL

About 70 percent of Israel's rain falls between November and March, with January and February being its rainiest months. Between June and August, there is often no rain at all. During January and February, snow sometimes falls in the central upland areas, including Jerusalem.

▶ The Jordan River flows from north to south through the Rift Valley, descending about 2,300 feet (700 m) over the course of its 186-mile (300-km) length. The river is usually narrow and shallow, but it swells during the winter rains.

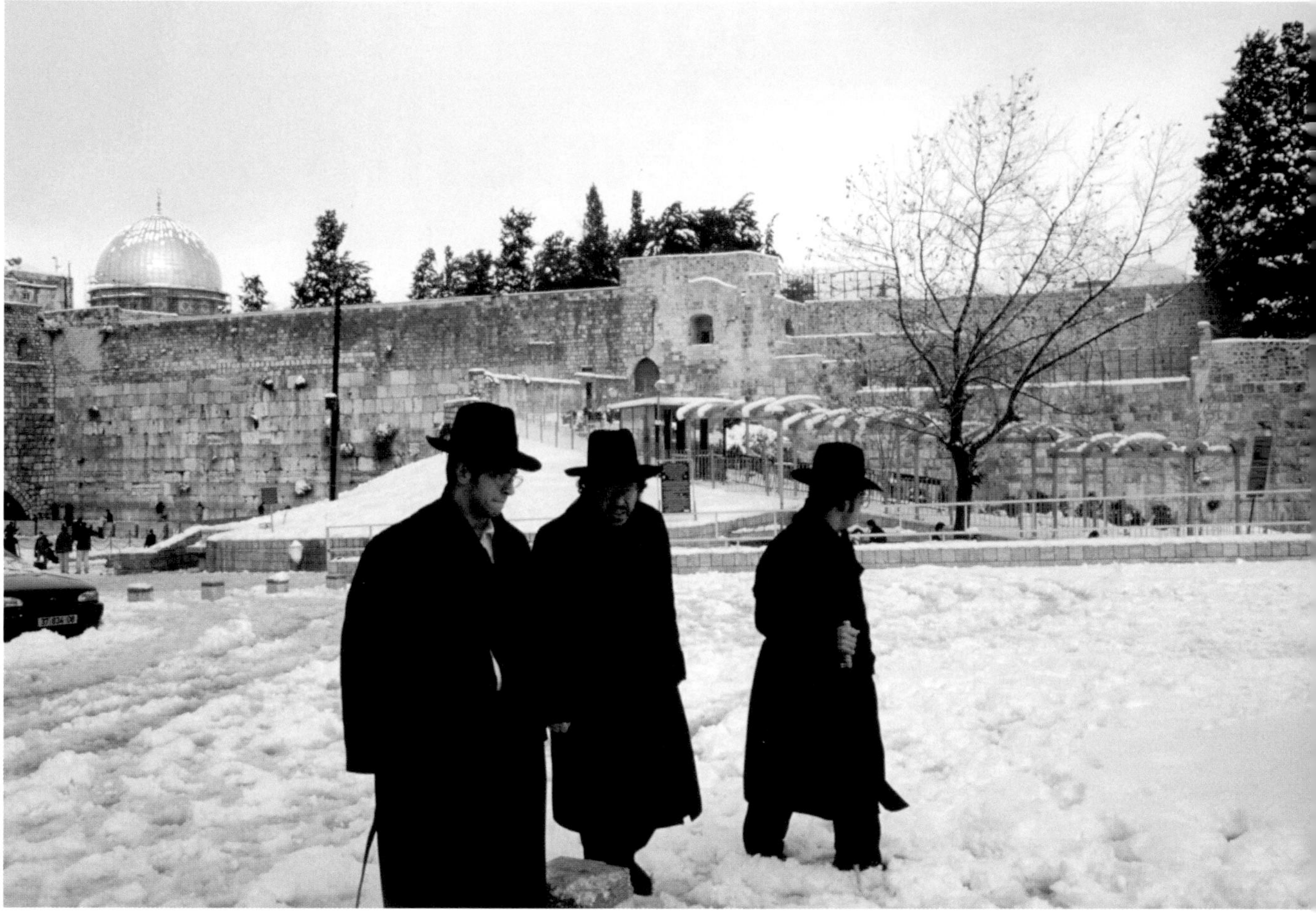

▲ With its relatively high altitude, Jerusalem experiences cold winters and occasional snowfalls.

In general, levels of rainfall diminish from north to south and from west to east. The mountainous parts of Galilee, in the north, receive an annual rainfall of about 40 inches (1,000 millimeters). The Judean Hills receive about 30 inches (700 mm), while the arid Negev receives only about 4 inches (100 mm). The driest spot, Elat, in the southern Negev, receives just 1 inch (25 mm) each year. When rain does fall in the Negev, it often comes in violent storms that can cause flash floods and erosion.

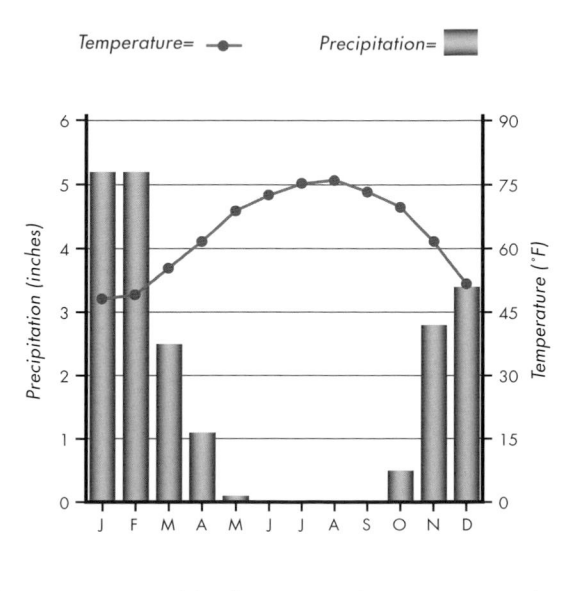

Temperature=
Precipitation=
Precipitation (inches)
Temperature (°F)
0
1
2
3
4
5
6
0
15
30
45
60
75
90
J F M A M J J A S O N D

▲ Average monthly climate conditions in Jerusalem

Did You Know?

Sixty percent of Israel's land is desert. Only 10 percent of Israel's population lives in its deserts.

CHAPTER 4

Population and Settlements

Today, Israel's population is nearly 6.7 million—compared to 806,000 in 1948, when the country was founded. Israel is densely populated, with 835.5 per sq mile (322.6 per sq km). Jews make up about 79 percent of the country's population, and Arabs make up most of the remaining 21 percent.

THE JEWISH POPULATION

Over one-third of the world's Jews live in Israel. Israel's government encourages Jews to move to Israel and, in 1950, the Knesset—Israel's parliament—passed the Law of Return, allowing any Jew to settle in Israel. About 2.75 million Jews have emigrated to Israel since 1948. The government provides temporary housing and job training to Jewish immigrants.

Jews have come to Israel from many different countries. Consequently, there are a number of separate ethnic groups within its Jewish population. Although they share important parts of their backgrounds, they have their own distinctive cultures, customs, and traditions. Israel's two main ethnic groups are Ashkenazic Jews and Sephardic Jews.

Population Data

- Population: 6.7 million
- Population 0–14 yrs: 27%
- Population 15–64 yrs: 63%
- Population 65+ yrs: 10%
- Population growth rate: 1.8%
- Population density: 835.5 per sq mile/ 322.6 per sq km
- Urban population: 92%
- Major cities: Tel Aviv-Yafo 3,025,000
    Haifa 948,000
    Jerusalem 690,000

Source: United Nations and World Bank

▶ A Sephardic Jewish family enjoys a picnic in a West Jerusalem park. They are celebrating Maimuna, a holiday that honors the Jewish thinker Moses Maimonides.

▲ A group of Druze women prepare for a wedding feast in Galilee. The Arabic-speaking Druze live in 22 villages in northern Israel.

Ashkenazic Jews originate from Central and Eastern Europe. They made up the majority of the Jewish population when Israel was founded, and their influence ensured that Israel developed into a Western-style liberal-democratic state. Sephardic Jews originate from the Middle East, North Africa, and the Mediterranean region. In Israel, Ashkenazic Jews tend to dominate the top positions in politics and business, while Sephardic Jews are more often at the lower end of the social and economic scale. However, the distinctions between these groups have become less important in recent years, because there are many Jews who have arrived in Israel from other areas or who grew up in the country.

THE ARAB POPULATION

About 1.3 million Arabs live in Israel. Most of them are descendants of Arabs who remained in the country after the founding of Israel. Muslims make up 77 percent of their number; 13 percent are Christian, and 10 percent are Druze and Bedouin. The Jewish and Arab communities have limited contact. Most Israeli Arabs live in separate areas, follow their own cultural traditions, and attend different schools.

Israeli Arabs have the same legal rights as Jews. However, tensions exist between the two communities. Many Israeli Arabs feel a strong bond with the Palestinian Arabs living in the West Bank and the Gaza Strip. They also claim that Arab population centers receive less financial help from the government than Jewish areas.

Focus on: The Many Languages of Israel

The official languages of Israel are Hebrew and Arabic. Most Israelis also speak English as a second language. The country's Jewish population speaks a modernized version of biblical Hebrew, while Arab Israelis speak Arabic. Although immigrants to Israel are instructed in Hebrew, many continue to use their native language at home. Russian is still spoken by the Russian immigrants who came to Israel in large numbers during the 1990s. Some older Ashkenazic Jews speak Yiddish, an eastern European language.

SETTLEMENTS

Israel's population is unevenly spread throughout the country. The Mediterranean coastal plain, with its fertile farmland and big cities, is the country's most densely populated area. The Negev Desert, located in Israel's south, is its least populated region.

Jewish immigration to the area that eventually became Israel had a major effect on settlement patterns in the region. Starting in the 1880s, Jewish immigrants settled on the Mediterranean coastal plain, the Judean foothills and the Jordan and Arava Valleys. Jerusalem and Haifa expanded rapidly in the early twentieth century, and Jewish settlers established Tel Aviv, a

suburb of the port of Yafo, in 1909. Jews became the majority in all these areas after many Palestinians fled in 1948. Today, Israel's Arab community is concentrated mainly in Galilee and in Jerusalem, where it makes up about 20 percent of the city's population.

URBAN CENTERS

Israel is a highly urbanized nation. More than one-half of its population lives within the metropolitan areas of its three major cities:

▼ An Orthodox Jewish man shops at the Mahane Yehuda Market in Jerusalem, as a soldier keeps watch. This market was the scene of a suicide bombing in 2002.

Jerusalem, Tel Aviv-Yafo, and Haifa. About 92 percent of the country's population lives in settlements of 2,000 people or more. Jerusalem lies in the Judean hills and covers 49 sq miles (126 sq km). It has a population of about 690,000. Tel Aviv-Yafo, on the Mediterranean coast, lies at the center of Israel's largest urban region, which covers 54 sq miles (150 sq km) and has a total population of more than 3 million. Tel Aviv-Yafo is Israel's commercial and industrial heartland. It is also an important center of culture and leisure. In the country's north is Haifa, which has Israel's largest port. Haifa also is an important industrial center. The main city in the Negev is Beersheba, which has a population of about 184,000.

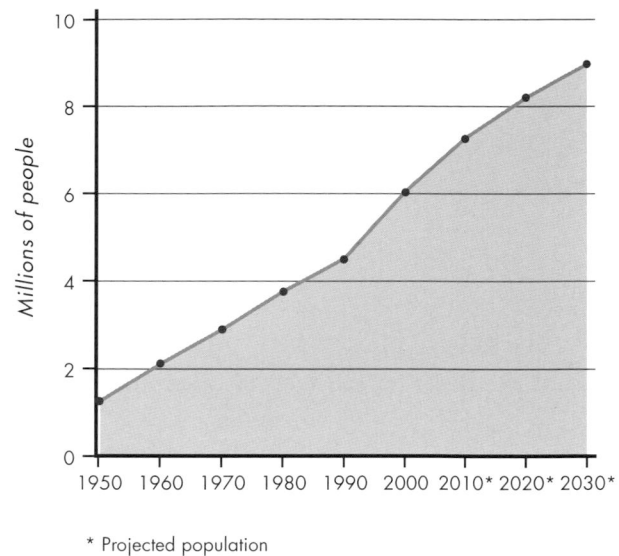

* Projected population

▲ Population growth 1950–2030

Focus on: Jerusalem

Jerusalem is one of the world's great cities, venerated by Jews, Christians, and Muslims alike. It contains many buildings and sites of religious and archaeological significance. Its walled "Old City" is divided into Muslim, Jewish, Christian, and Armenian quarters, reflecting the city's links to different ethnic and religious groups. As the capital of ancient Israel, Jerusalem is Judaism's most sacred city. As the place where Jesus was put to death, it is a place of Christian pilgrimage. And as the location from which the Prophet Muhammad is believed to have ascended to heaven, Jerusalem is also holy to Muslims. Between 1949 and 1967, the city was divided into Israeli West Jerusalem and Jordanian East Jerusalem. Israel captured East Jerusalem in the Six-Day War and reaffirmed that Jerusalem was its capital in 1980. This claim is disputed by the UN, and the status of the city remains a source of conflict between Israel and the Palestinians.

▲ Arab Muslim women pray outside the Dome of the Rock, located in Jerusalem, during the festival of Ramadan.

CHAPTER 5

Government and Politics

▲ This large bronze menorah stands outside the Knesset building in Jerusalem. A menorah is a Jewish ceremonial candleholder.

Israel is a democratic republic. It has no written constitution. Instead the rules of its government are laid down in a series of basic laws. Israel has a parliamentary system of government in which a number of parties, representing a wide range of opinions, compete for influence by winning seats in the country's parliament, the Knesset.

THE KNESSET

The Knesset is a single-chamber parliament. It has 120 members, each elected for a maximum term of four years. The role of the Knesset is to debate and vote on legislation, approve budgets and taxes, elect the president, and conduct votes of confidence or no confidence in the prime minister and the cabinet.

THE EXECUTIVE

The prime minister is the most powerful figure in Israeli politics. He or she is head of Israel's government and, usually, the leader of the majority party in the Knesset. The prime minister forms and heads the cabinet, the country's main policy-making body; decides on the topics of cabinet meetings; and has the final say on policy decisions. The cabinet, also often called the government, puts forward legislation which is then voted on by the Knesset. Knesset committees and individuals can also put forward legislation. Legislation is passed by

Focus on: Israel's Justice System

The Israeli justice system has both secular and religious courts. The president appoints judges for both types of court. Secular courts deal with most criminal and civil cases. The country's highest secular court is the Supreme Court, which hears appeals from lower courts in civil and criminal cases. The Supreme Court is a powerful institution. It can declare actions of Israel's government illegal if it regards them as contrary to Knesset legislation. The country's religious courts hear cases regarding personal matters such as marriage, divorce, adoption, guardianship, and inheritance. Each religious community has its own religious courts.

Israel's head of state is the country's president. The president of Israel holds little political power and performs mainly ceremonial functions. Israel's president does, however, have the power to appoint certain important national officials, including judges and the governor of the Bank of Israel.

a simple majority. Israel's cabinet may have as many as 18 ministers, at least half of whom must be from the Knesset. Each minister is in charge of a government department, such as the Ministry of Finance, the Ministry of Health, or the Ministry of Transportation.

LOCAL GOVERNMENT

Israel is divided into six local government districts—Central, Jerusalem, Haifa, Northern, Southern, and Tel Aviv—and into 15 subdistricts. The Minister of the Interior appoints and oversees district officials. District officials oversee the elected councils that run each district. Municipal councils serve the larger cities, while local councils govern smaller settlements. Regional rural councils look after rural areas. Councils are responsible for providing education, health, sanitation, and welfare services, as well as maintaining roads, public parks, and public buildings. They also set and collect local taxes.

◀ The Knesset meets for at least eight months each year. The sessions are presided over by a member called the Speaker and are open to the media and the public.

ראש הממשלה
אריאל שרון

POLITICAL PARTIES

Israel has a large number of political parties, representing a wide variety of views. Secular parties represent political viewpoints ranging from left-wing socialist to right-wing capitalist. The country also has religious parties that appeal particularly to either the Sephardic or Ashkenazic Jewish communities. Several Arab parties also compete for representation.

In spite of its many parties, Israel's political scene is dominated by two: Labor and Likud. Labor is a socialist party, supporting a welfare state and government control of the economy. It is in favor of a secular state, equal rights for minorities, and a negotiated settlement between Israel and the Palestinians. Likud is a nationalist, right-of-center party that believes in free enterprise, retaining the occupied territories, and a more aggressive approach to foreign affairs and security matters. Neither party has ever achieved an absolute majority in the Knesset. As a result, they are able to rule

▲ Ehud Olmert became Israel's acting prime minister after Prime Minister Ariel Sharon (whose empty chair he is sitting next to) suffered a massive stroke in January 2006. On April 14, 2006, Olmert became the country's interim prime minister.

only with the support of smaller parties. The small parties, especially the religious parties, therefore wield considerable power.

In November 2005, Israeli prime minister Ariel Sharon resigned from Likud in order to start a new centrist party called Kadima (Forward). Sharon was a popular leader and looked capable, with his new party, of ending the dominance of Labor and Likud in Israeli politics. On January 4, 2006, however, Sharon suffered a stroke, and his deputy, Ehud Olmert, became acting prime minister. In the March 2006 national elections, Kadima won 29 seats, making it the largest party in the Knesset and enabling it to form a government with the help of other smaller parties.

THE WEST BANK

The West Bank—the territory on the west bank of the Jordan River that has been occupied by Israel since 1967—is not a part of Israel, but it remains under Israeli military control. The area was also under Israeli civilian control between 1967 and 1994. Under the terms of the Oslo Accords (1993), Israel began handing civilian control of parts of the West Bank over to the newly created Palestinian Authority (PA). Between 1994 and 1999, Israel handed over 29 percent of the West Bank, including most Palestinian population centers, to the PA. In these areas, the PA collects taxes and is responsible for providing education, social services, law enforcement, and health care. Israel has retained control of the armed forces, foreign affairs, and movements between Palestinian areas on the West Bank. The people living in the PA-controlled West Bank are not Israeli citizens and cannot vote in Israel's elections. Following the death of Yasser Arafat, politics in the PA grew complex, with Hamas, a terrorist group, gaining a great deal of power.

Focus on: Israel's Electoral System

All Israeli citizens over the age of 18 can vote in elections. In national elections, the whole country is one constituency. Citizens vote not for individual candidates but for political parties. Parties must receive at least 1.5 percent of the vote to gain a seat in the Knesset. The number of candidates elected from a party depends on the percentage of the total vote that the party receives. Each party prepares ranked lists of its candidates. The top-ranked candidates are the ones that become members of the Knesset, depending on the percentage of the vote won by the party. This is called the party list system.

▼ Arab Israeli women vote in an Israeli national election. Most Arab Israelis tend to vote for Arab parties, which won 10 seats in the Knesset in the 2006 election.

CHAPTER 6

Energy and Resources

Israel is not rich in energy sources. It relies on imported oil and coal to meet most of its needs. Water is also a scarce resource in the country, forcing Israel to adopt new and innovative methods of extracting water. The country has reasonable supplies of minerals, especially in the Dead Sea area. Israel has greatly expanded its agricultural output since 1948 and now produces most of its own food.

ENERGY

Israel has very limited amounts of oil, natural gas, and oil shale, and almost all of its energy is provided by imported oil and coal. Most of its oil comes from Egypt and Mexico, while its coal comes from South Africa, Australia, and Britain. Its electricity is generated mainly by coal- and oil-burning power stations. The government has encouraged the supply of electric power to rural areas by providing electricity at low prices.

Israel has also looked at alternative sources of energy. The Israel Atomic Energy Commission was set up in 1952, and small atomic reactors were built south of Tel Aviv and in the Negev Desert for nuclear research. Israel has pioneered research into solar energy, especially the use of solar panels for home water heating.

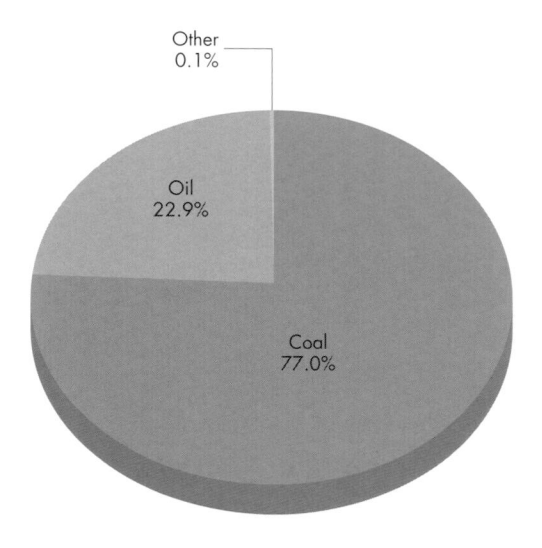

▲ Electricity production by type

◀ These solar panels in the Negev are part of a research project at Ben-Gurion University's Jacob Blaustein Institute for Desert Research. The goal of the project is to provide large-scale solar power stations in the future.

Energy Data

- Energy consumption as % of world total: 0.2%
- Energy consumption by sector (% of total):

    Industry: 24.1%

    Transportation: 31.7%

    Agriculture: 1.1%

    Services: 7.6%

    Residential: 17.2%

    Other: 18.3%
- CO_2 emissions as % of world total: 0.3%
- CO_2 emissions per capita in tons per year: 11.5

Source: World Resources Institute

WATER

With an average of just six months of rainfall per year and large areas of desert, Israel has always struggled to fulfill its water needs. The country's main water sources are the Jordan River; the Sea of Galilee (Lake Kinneret); and a few small river systems, natural springs, and underground water tables. This provides total yearly water resources of 60 billion cubic feet (1.7 billion cubic meters). About 65 percent of this water is used for irrigation and the rest for industrial and domestic use.

Because of Israel's shortage of freshwater sources, the country has developed several innovative techniques to increase or make more efficient use of its water supply. These techniques include the purification of sewage water for use in irrigation; cloud seeding (scattering chemicals into clouds from an aircraft to cause rain); and desalination (removal of salt) of seawater. The country's biggest

Focus on: The National Water Carrier

The National Water Carrier, completed in 1964, is a network of giant pipes, aqueducts, canals, reservoirs, tunnels, dams, and pumping stations that runs through Israel. Its job is to bring water from the north and central regions to Israel's arid south. It supplies a total of 35 billion cubic feet (1 billion cubic meters) of water annually.

▼ Many farmers in Israel use the drip irrigation system, shown here in use in the Negev Desert. Because this system delivers water directly to crop roots, there is very little waste or evaporation. The system allows the amount of watering to be varied according to soil type and the slope of the terrain.

desalination plant is in Elat, and it provides 459 million cubic feet (13 million cubic meters) of drinkable water annually. Efficient use of water in irrigation has been greatly advanced by drip irrigation, a method pioneered by the Israeli Simcha Blass and his son in 1959, which delivers water directly to the root systems of crops.

? Did You Know?

In 2004, Israel signed an agreement with Turkey to import water in giant tankers across the Mediterranean Sea.

▼ Sprinklers water crops on a farm in the Negev Desert. Extensive water supply and irrigation projects have succeeded in bringing large parts of this desert area under cultivation.

MINERAL RESOURCES

The Dead Sea is Israel's chief source of minerals. Potash (used mainly in fertilizers), bromine, magnesium, and table salt are all mined in this area. Phosphates, copper, bromine, clay, and gypsum are mined in the Negev Desert. Israel is the world's leading exporter of bromine. Copper is also mined in Arava, and some marble is quarried in Galilee.

AGRICULTURE AND FISHING

Since it was founded, Israel has greatly expanded the amount of its land available for farming through an extensive system of irrigation. Today, about 35.8 percent of Israel's land is under cultivation—more than three times the cultivated area in 1948. About 44 percent of this cultivated land is irrigated. Israel's main crops are citrus fruits, peanuts,

Focus on: Kibbutzim and Moshavim

Many of Israel's rural Jews live on kibbutzim and moshavim. A kibbutz is a community in which the residents own the wealth and property collectively. Kibbutzim were originally agricultural communities, although many of them now engage in industry, services, and tourism. The members receive their basic needs of clothing, food, and shelter in exchange for their labor. Any profits remaining after members have been provided for are invested in the community. The kibbutz movement is unique to Israel. The first kibbutzim were founded in the early twentieth century. Their democratic and socialist character had a strong influence on the development of Israeli society. Today, Israel has 268 kibbutzim, with a total population of about 113,000 living on them.

A moshav is a farming community in which each family works its land and lives separately while cooperating in both the buying of equipment and supplies and the marketing and selling of their produce. Today, Israel has about 450 moshavim, with a total population of about 189,000.

◀ A worker at Moshav Neot Hakikar, located in the Negev, with some newly harvested cantaloupes.

sugar beets, cotton, cereals, tomatoes, avocados, potatoes, eggs, grain, poultry, dairy products, and flowers.

In addition to irrigation, mechanization has also dramatically helped to increase Israel's agricultural output. Only 2 percent of Israel's workforce is employed on farms, because much of the farm work is now performed by machines. Income from food exports covers the cost of any food Israel needs to import. With all of its water resources fully exploited, further expansion of agriculture in Israel will depend on developing new techniques such as cloud seeding and desalination of seawater.

There are only limited quantities of fish off Israel's Mediterranean and Red Sea coasts, so Israel relies on richer fishing grounds in the Indian and Atlantic Oceans to meet demand. Israel also raises freshwater fish in inland artificial fishponds, mainly in its north.

CHAPTER 7

Economy and Income

Israel has had to face unique challenges in its short history that have often hampered its ability to build a successful economy. Constant threats to its security have necessitated a great deal of spending on defense, and the country has also faced the problems of housing and finding jobs for large numbers of immigrants. The government has had to impose high taxes in order to pay for these things. Israel also suffers from a lack of natural resources and, for much of its history, economic isolation from surrounding Arab states.

For these reasons, Israel's government has always played an important role in planning, supporting, and intervening in the country's economy. The government is also the country's largest employer, particularly in the public services sector. In the 1980s, to help stimulate economic growth and reduce government spending, Israel began privatizing many of its government-run businesses. However, by 2004, the public sector still represented about 55 percent of Israel's Gross Domestic Product (GDP), with privately owned companies accounting for 45 percent of the country's GDP.

ECONOMIC EXPANSION

In spite of challenges, Israel's economy has expanded greatly since 1948, thanks to the influx of professionals and skilled laborers from Europe and North America; financial aid from

▼ A worker on a production line at a pharmaceutical (medical drug) factory in Israel. Israel's pharmaceutical industry generates sales of about U.S.$1.25 billion per year and employs about 5,400 people.

◀ A diamond inspector at the National Diamond Center in Jerusalem. Israel's diamond exports were worth around U.S.$9 billion in 2003.

Western countries, especially the United States; and government investment in research and development. Today, most Israelis enjoy a high standard of living. Foreign investments grew from U.S.$175 million in 1987 to U.S.$3.7 billion in 2003. Industrial exports almost tripled between 1991 and 2003, increasing from U.S.$10.9 billion to U.S.$28.4 billion.

Israel has also largely overcome many of the economic problems that beset it during the 1980s and 1990s. Inflation, which was as high as 445 percent in the 1980s, was just over 1 percent in 2005. Foreign debt, which was 25 percent of Israel's GDP in 1995, has now disappeared. The country's trade deficit (the difference between imports and exports) fell from U.S.$7.8 billion in 1995 to U.S.$3 billion in 2004.

SERVICE INDUSTRIES

Israel has a very big service sector. It contributes about 75 percent of the nation's GDP. A large proportion of workers in this sector are employed by the government or by government-owned businesses. A major area of activity is providing services such as housing, education, and training for the country's large immigrant population. The government is Israel's largest employer, although it has privatized many of its businesses it ran. Other important service industries in the country include business and financial services, retail, transportation, communication services, and tourism.

Economic Data

- Gross National Income (GNI) in U.S.$: 118,123,503,616
- World rank by GNI: 36
- GNI per capita in U.S.$: 17,380
- World rank by GNI per capita: 40
- Economic growth: 4%

Source: World Bank

? Did You Know?

Based in Tel Aviv, Israel's diamond-cutting and diamond-polishing industry, is the largest in the world. It is responsible for the polishing of 40 percent of the world's diamonds, and it produces about 80 percent of the world's small polished diamonds, which are used in jewelry.

MANUFACTURING

Israel's manufacturing sector is the most diversified and technologically advanced in the Middle East. It has benefited from major government investment since 1948. In 1973, the government set up the Office of the Chief Scientist (OCS) to provide financial assistance to companies for research and development into new products. Today, the OCS gives out about U.S.$400 million annually in research and development grants.

Traditional manufacturing industries in Israel included food processing, textiles, chemical products, drugs, fertilizers, paper, and plastics. Since the 1980s, Israel has also become a leading manufacturer of high-technology products such as telecommunications equipment, computer hardware and software, weapons systems, and electronic equipment.

INTERNATIONAL TRADE

With few natural resources, Israel has imported more than it exports every year since 1948. In 2004, its total exports amounted to about U.S.$34 billion, while its imports totaled nearly U.S.$37 billion, leaving a trade deficit of about U.S.$3 billion. Between 1948 and 2002, Israel required a total of about U.S.$170 billion to cover all of its annual trade deficits. About two-thirds of this sum was paid for by donations from Jewish organizations around the world; by immigrants; and by grants from foreign governments, especially the United States. The rest was paid for by borrowing from individuals, banks, and foreign governments. Israel has been repaying these loans since its earliest years.

Israel's main trading partners are the European Union (EU) and the United States. Its chief imports include chemicals, grain, iron, steel, petroleum products, rough diamonds, and textiles. Its chief exports are chemical products, citrus fruits, electronic equipment, fertilizers, polished diamonds, clothing, and processed foods.

THE WORKFORCE

In 2004, Israel's workforce was 2.68 million, 42.2 percent of whom were women. The country's largest employment sector is public services, followed by manufacturing, retail and wholesale trade, and financial and business services.

The workforce includes about 250,000 Israeli Arabs. It also includes about 100,000 foreign laborers, from places such as China, Thailand,

◄ Cargo that is ready for export is loaded onto a container ship at the Israeli port of Haifa. With its relatively small domestic market, Israel's economy relies mainly on exports for its growth.

the Philippines, South America, Turkey, and eastern Europe. These people work mainly in agriculture and construction. Foreign workers have replaced large numbers of Palestinian workers from the occupied territories, many of whom have been banned from working in Israel since the first intifada (1987–1993). Unemployment was 10.7 percent in 2004.

HAVES AND HAVE NOTS

Israel's economic success has led to a high standard of living for most Israeli citizens. However, progress has not been uniform throughout society. Many of the country's Sephardic Jews, who arrived in large numbers in the decades following independence, found it hard to adapt to Israel's predominantly Ashkenazic culture. Ashkenazic Jews, with their European backgrounds, benefited from Western-style education, and were, therefore, at an advantage over the Sephardic Jews when competing for top jobs in government, the media, and industry. Consequently, Sephardic communities tend to be poorer than average. Israeli Arab communities are also generally at the lower end of the economic scale.

> ### Focus on: The Histadrut
>
> The Histadrut (the General Federation of Labor) was established in 1920 as an umbrella organization of trade unions to represent Israel's workers. Today, the Histadrut includes 78 trade unions that look after the interests of 700,000 Israeli employees. These people work in every area of the Israeli economy, including tourism, manufacturing, education, law, and journalism. In addition to negotiating with employers on workers' wages and conditions, the Histadrut offers its members health insurance and educational and recreational services.

▼ A homeless man begs in front of a clothing store in Tel Aviv. Poverty is becoming a serious problem in Israel. In 2003, almost one out of five families lived on less than U.S.$1,000 per month.

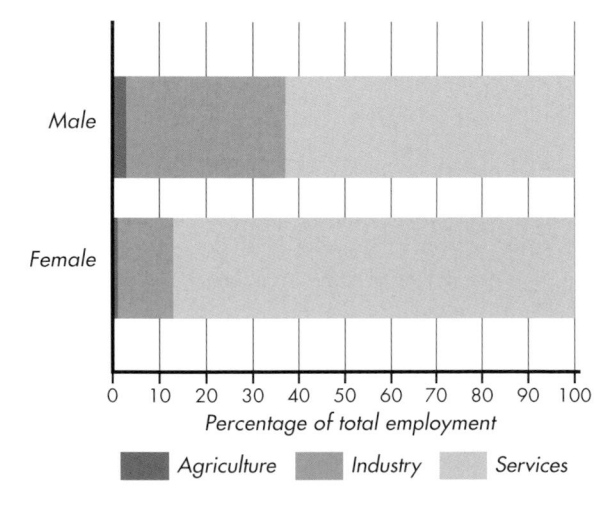

Percentage of total employment

■ Agriculture   ■ Industry   ■ Services

▲ Labor force by sector and gender

CHAPTER 8

Global Connections

Israel's relations with the international community, especially since 1967, have often been strained. The country has been criticized frequently, including, for example, for the building of settlements in the occupied territories and, since 2002, for the construction of its security fence. In spite of these controversies, Israel maintains relations with the majority of countries around the world—160 out of 191. Since the peace process began with the Madrid conference in October 1991, 68 nations have established relations, or renewed lapsed relations, with Israel.

INTERNATIONAL ORGANIZATIONS

Israel is a member of many international organizations, including the United Nations (UN), the International Atomic Energy Agency (IAEA), the World Health Organization (WHO), the World Bank, and the International Monetary Fund (IMF). Israel is excluded from a number of regional organizations in the Middle East, including the Organization of the Islamic Conference and the Arab League.

Israel has had an up-and-down relationship with the UN since it joined in 1949. UN resolutions in 1967 and 1973 called upon Arab states to recognize Israel's right to exist, and in 1998, the UN General Assembly passed a resolution acknowledging that anti-Semitism (hatred of Jews) is a form of racism. On the other hand, hundreds of UN resolutions have been critical of Israel. In 1967, UN Resolution 242 called upon Israel to withdraw from territories it seized during the Six-Day War. (The resolution also called for all states in the area to respect the political independence and territorial integrity of every other state.) And, in 1975, the UN General Assembly adopted a resolution that called Zionism a form of racism.

▶ An Ethiopian Jewish woman with her baby at her Jerusalem home. She is one of about 10,000 Ethiopian Jews, known as Falashas, who were brought to Israel in two air-rescue operations. The first was during a famine in 1984, and the second was during political unrest in 1991.

This resolution was repealed in 1991. Israel has played an active part in the UN. It is a member of the UN Educational, Scientific, and Cultural Organization (UNESCO), the UN Office of the High Commissioner for Refugees (UNHCR), and the Food and Agriculture Organization (FAO).

OTHER COUNTRIES

Historically, Israel has had especially close ties with the United States, due in part to the large Jewish-American population, as well as the fact that the two countries share similar liberal-democratic values. Israel also has strong connections with Europe. Many of the original Jewish settlers to Palestine came from Central

▶ Former prime minister of Israel Ariel Sharon shakes hands with UN secretary-general Kofi Annan during their meeting in 2005. Annan was hoping to revive the stalled peace plan to create a Palestinian Arab state.

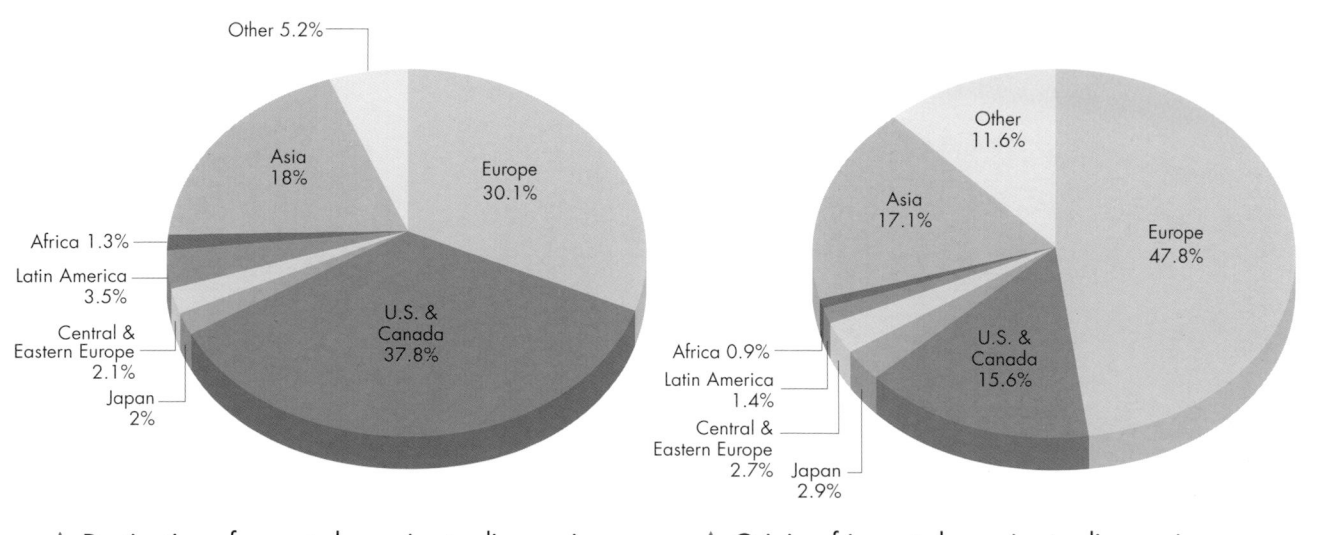

Export pie chart labels:
Other 5.2%
Asia 18%
Africa 1.3%
Latin America 3.5%
Central & Eastern Europe 2.1%
Japan 2%
U.S. & Canada 37.8%
Europe 30.1%

Import pie chart labels:
Other 11.6%
Asia 17.1%
Africa 0.9%
Latin America 1.4%
Central & Eastern Europe 2.7%
Japan 2.9%
U.S. & Canada 15.6%
Europe 47.8%

▲ Destination of exports by major trading region   ▲ Origin of imports by major trading region

and Eastern Europe. Consequently Israel has deep historical and cultural links with continental Europe. Western Europe is also Israel's leading trading partner.

Israel had five major wars with its Arab neighbors between 1948 and 1982. However, relations with several Arab states have improved in recent decades. Peace treaties have been negotiated with Egypt (1979) and Jordan (1994). Diplomatic ties were established with Morocco, Mauritania, and Tunisia in 1994, and trade representation offices opened in Qatar and Oman in 1996. Morocco, Tunisia, and Oman, however, broke off official relations with Israel after the beginning of the second intifada.

MASHAV

In 1958, Israel launched the Center for International Cooperation, or MASHAV, a program that aims to share technology and expertise with developing countries around the world. Since then, almost 200,000 people from about 140 countries have undergone MASHAV

► An female Israeli athlete runs with a flag during the opening ceremony of the 16th Maccabiah Games in 2001. The Games were almost cancelled because of security fears associated with the recently erupted second intifada.

Focus on: The "Jewish Olympics"

The Maccabiah Games is an athletic festival that takes place in Israel every four years. The best Jewish athletes from all over the world, as well as Israelis of all religions, are invited to compete in a range of sports. The idea of a Jewish athletic competition was conceived by a 15-year-old Russian-born Jew named Yosef Yekutieli in 1912. The first Maccabiah Games took place in 1932 in the British Mandate of Palestine. A second competition was organized in 1935. After the Games were suspended during World War II and during the 1948–1949 war, the third Maccabiah Games took place in the new state of Israel in 1950. Since 1953, the games have taken place every four years. At the 17th Maccabiah Games, held in July 2005, about 7,000 athletes from 55 countries competed, ranking it (in terms of numbers of participants) among the five largest sporting gatherings in the world. Competing countries include the United States, Canada, Mexico, Brazil, the Netherlands, Germany, Argentina, South Africa, Australia, Britain, and Switzerland.

WORLD JEWRY

Millions of Jews from all over the world regard Israel as central to Jewish life. For its part, Israel has always sought to strengthen its links with Jewish communities in different parts of the world. It does this through two organizations, the World Zionist Organization (WZO) and the Jewish Agency for Israel (JAFI).

The WZO was set up in 1897 with the aim of helping Jews return to their ancient homeland in Palestine. Its primary aim was achieved in 1948 with the creation of the state of Israel. JAFI was founded in 1929 by the WZO to deal with foreign governments and international organizations on behalf of the Jewish community in Palestine. Since 1948, both the WZO and JAFI have continued to help Jews to emigrate to Israel and to assist them in finding housing, education, and employment once they have arrived. The organizations also encourage Jewish education in Jewish communities and defend the rights of Jews worldwide.

training courses. MASHAV focuses on fields in which Israel has developed particular expertise. These fields include water resource management, irrigation, desert agriculture, combating desertification, emergency and disaster medicine, refugee absorption, early childhood education, community development, and many others.

MASHAV offers almost 300 courses per year, both in Israel and abroad. It also often sends expert consultants to offer short- or long-term guidance to individual countries who wish to put into practice what students from those countries have learned in the courses. Demonstration farms have been built in several countries to show how good agricultural practices pioneered in Israel can be maintained over a long period.

MASHAV also offers practical medical expertise. For example, it sends Israeli eye doctors to many developing countries to set up temporary "eye camps" in which they treat preventable blindness and eye diseases.

▶ A Jewish family from Baltimore, Maryland, prepares to emigrate to their new home in Jerusalem. The family has been assisted by Nefesh B'Nefesh, an organization that helps Jews with the process of relocating to Israel and finding homes, jobs, and schools when they get there.

CHAPTER 9

Transportation and Communications

Israel has a modern, efficient transportation system. This system was developed during Israel's early years, partly to help move troops and equipment swiftly around the country as it defended itself from its hostile neighbors.

ROADS

Most private and commercial transportation in Israel is by road. As of 2002, Israel had 10,711 miles (17,237 km) of urban and rural roads, connecting almost every part of the country. Road-building, however, has failed to keep pace with population growth and the rise in the number of cars. Israel now has about 1.54 million vehicles on its roads—an average of about 144 cars for every mile of road (89 per km), compared to 65 cars for every mile of road (40 per km) in the United States.

The government is attempting to tackle the problem of congestion by building more roads and also by trying to encourage people to use buses and trains. There are an increasing number of bus-only routes within cities.

RAILWAYS

Israel has about 398 miles (640 km) of railway lines, all of which are run by the government-owned company Israel Railways. More than 200 passenger trains and 100 freight trains run each day through the country. However, the number of people traveling by train is still very small

▼ A road snakes down a mountainside near Mitzpe Ramon, located in the Negev. The emptiness of this desert road contrasts with the growing congestion of Israel's urban routes.

◄ Passengers wait to board an El Al airliner at Ben Gurion Airport. El Al was owned by the government of Israel until it was privatized in 2003.

compared to the number of people using cars. Israel's government hopes to encourage commuters to travel by rail by upgrading and expanding its network. Light-rail networks are being built in Jerusalem, Tel Aviv, Beersheba, and Haifa to relieve traffic congestion and pollution in city centers. The largest network, in Tel Aviv, will include underground sections in the busiest parts of the city.

AVIATION

Israel's international airline, El Al, was founded in 1948. In October 2005, El Al had a fleet of 34 planes that carried over 3 million passengers per year to and from 43 destinations in North America, Europe, and parts of Africa and Asia. Arkia Israel Airlines, founded in 1950, is Israel's domestic airline. It serves destinations within Israel and various locations in Europe and the Mediterranean. Israel's main international airport is Ben Gurion Airport, in Lod, near Tel Aviv. It handles about 10 million travelers each year. The country has smaller airports at Atarot (near Jerusalem), Rosh Pinna, Haifa, and Elat.

? Did You Know?

Egged, Israel's national bus carrier, is the second-largest bus operator in the world, after London Transport. It provides 70 percent of Israel's public transportation. Founded in 1933, Egged today runs 4,000 buses on thousands of routes. Each day it carries about one million passengers—almost one-sixth of Israel's population.

Transport & Communications Data

- Total roads: 10,711 miles/17,237 km
- Total paved roads: 10,711 miles/17,237 km
- Total unpaved roads: 0 km/0 miles
- Total railways: 398 miles/640 km
- Airports: 28
- Cars per 1,000 people: 230
- Cellular phones per 1,000 people: 961
- Personal computers per 1,000 people: 243
- Internet users per 1,000 people: 301

Source: World Bank and CIA World Factbook

SHIPPING

Until 1978, Israel had no trade relations with its neighboring countries. Because even today its trade with the adjoining Arab states is very small, shipping has always been vital to Israel's economy. Almost 99 percent of Israeli exports pass through its three major ports at Haifa, Ashdod, and Elat. Haifa Port, built in the 1930s, is Israel's oldest and largest port. It has modern facilities capable of handling all types of cargo, and it processes about 19 million tons (17.2 million metric tons) of cargo and over 400,000 passengers annually. Israel's national container shipping company, Zim Israel Navigation, is the tenth largest in the world. It operates a fleet of over 81 vessels that call at 265 ports around the world.

THE MEDIA

About one out of four adult Israelis owns a television and one out of two owns a radio. Israel has four television networks. One of these is state-owned, and the other three are commercial networks. The Israeli Broadcasting Authority runs the country's state-owned radio and TV stations. The country also has three cable TV broadcasters. By 2004, cable television was available to 97 percent of Israel's homes, and there were about 1 million subscribers.

Israel is one of the few countries to design, build, launch, and operate its own satellites. The first was AMOS, launched in 1996. DBS (Direct Broadcast Satellite) TV is operated by a company called Yes, and it has about 400,000 subscribers. It also broadcasts to the rest of the Middle East, North Africa, and Eastern Europe. Many Arab Israelis watch television broadcasts from neighboring countries.

Israel has 34 daily newspapers. About half of these are in Hebrew and the other half are in other languages, including Arabic and English. Well-known newspapers include the *Jerusalem Post*, *Ha'aretz*, and *Ma'ariv*. Over one thousand magazines are also published in Israel.

TELECOMMUNICATIONS

Israel has one of the most highly developed telecommunications

◄ Young Israelis chat on their cellular phones in Jerusalem. Israel has four main cellular-phone service providers, all of which cover the entire country.

networks in the Middle East, and citizens have been quick to embrace the latest technological advances. Israel has 6.4 million cellular phones —nearly one for every person—and 3 million land-line phones. Israel also has one of the highest rates of Internet use in the world. The Internet is now used in more than 50 percent of Israeli households and 70 percent of Israeli businesses. Between 2003 and 2004, the number of high-speed Internet connections in Israel grew by 200 percent to 920,000, bringing high-speed Internet to 43 percent of Israel's homes.

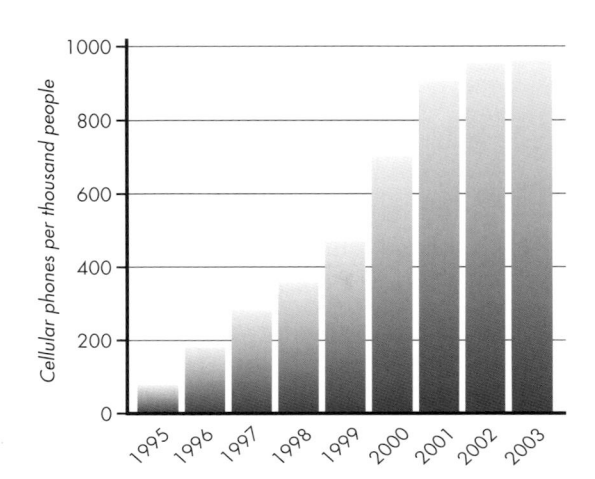

▲ Cellular phone use, 1995–2003

Focus on: The Postal Service

Despite the growing adoption of modern technology, millions of Israelis continue to write letters rather than send e-mails. About 2 million items of mail are handled by the Israel Postal Authority (ISA) every day. They are fed through 700 post offices around the country. The ISA employs 2,000 delivery people, and has computerized links with about 30 countries.

▼ Israelis going online in an Internet café in Jerusalem's Old City. All the main towns and tourist centers in Israel have Internet cafés.

CHAPTER 10

Education and Health

Education is very important in Jewish culture, and it is given high priority in Israel. This is reflected in the high literacy rate of Israeli citizens. The country's educational system has had to face the challenge of absorbing Jewish immigrant children from many different cultural backgrounds.

SCHOOLS

In Israel, education for 5- to 18-year-olds is free, and it is compulsory for 5- to 16-year-olds. About 90 percent of Israel's children complete their compulsory education. The country has different types of schools for each community. Jewish children can attend government-funded secular or religious schools, where they are taught in Hebrew. Both types of school offer a similar range of subjects, but the religious schools give more attention to Jewish studies. The Israeli curriculum places special emphasis on agricultural and technological training. Some of the country's high schools specialize in these areas.

Many Orthodox Jews, who follow the traditional rules of Judaism, send their children to private religious schools where they are given more intensive religious instruction. Arab and Druze children attend government-funded schools where they are taught in Arabic about their history, religion, and culture.

HIGHER EDUCATION

After completing their high-school education, Israelis have a choice of university, vocational, or other adult education. Most high-school graduates

◀ These children are in a classroom in an Israeli school that offers a mixture of secular and religious education. Israeli schools can choose from a wide range of subjects within a curriculum laid down by the Ministry of Education.

do their compulsory military service (three years for men; two years for women) before entering higher education at an average age of 21. Well over half of Israelis aged between 20 and 24 are enrolled in one of the country's institutions of post-secondary or higher education.

Well-known universities in Israel include the Hebrew University of Jerusalem; Bar-Ilan University, a religious university in Ramat Gan; Tel Aviv University; the University of Haifa; Technion-Israel Institute of Technology, in Haifa; and Ben-Gurion University, in Beersheba. Students in isolated areas can learn from a distance through the Open University in Tel Aviv-Yafo, founded in 1974. Adult immigrants arrive in Israel with varying levels of education and literacy. The country has adult education courses open to them, aimed at different abilities. Subjects include Hebrew, art, and music, as well as vocational training in nursing, teaching, or architecture.

Education and Health Data

- Life expectancy at birth, male: 77
- Life expectancy at birth, female: 81
- Infant mortality rate per 1,000: 5
- Under five mortality rate per 1,000: 6
- Physicians per 1,000 people: 4
- Health expenditure as % of GDP: 9%
- Education expenditure as % of GDP: 8%
- Primary school net enrollment: 100%
- Student-teacher ratio, primary: 15
- Adult literacy as % age 15+: 97%

Source: United Nations Agencies and World Bank

Focus on: Educational Television

School and university education in Israel is supplemented by a government-provided service of educational TV programs, called ETV (Educational Television). Program-makers consult with schools and universities in developing new teaching methods. The programs cater to different audiences, including preschoolers, teenagers, and adults. They are designed for use in the classroom or at home. ETV is broadcast on two channels six days a week for about ten hours each day.

◄ Young Israeli boys learn their lessons at a yeshiva in northern Israel. A yeshiva is an Orthodox Jewish school that provides instruction in the Jewish scholarly tradition.

Focus on: Critical Care

Sadly, Israeli surgeons have had to deal with many terrorist incidents. They have built up internationally recognized expertise in the management and treatment of terrorist bomb victims, which they offer to other countries. They make recommendations on how to treat common bomb-blast injuries, including brain, lung, bone, and stomach injuries. These injuries, challenging on their own, often occur in combination in bombing victims. Israeli specialists in critical care also suggest ways of managing hospital intensive care units following a terrorist incident.

▲ Israeli soldiers and paramedics rush a wounded boy to hospital following an attack by a gunman in August 2005. Israeli medical professionals are experienced in dealing with critical injuries such as these.

HEALTH CARE

Israel ranks among the most successful countries in the world in terms of its high life expectancy and its low rate of infant mortality. Israel's life expectancy is 77 years for men and 81 years for women. The country's under five mortality rate is 6 per 1,000 (compared to 8 per 1,000 in the United States).

Basic medical care, including hospitalization, is offered to all Israeli citizens through a national health insurance program. All working citizens pay up to 4.8 percent of their income to the National Insurance Institute to fund health care. The population is served by a large network of hospitals, out-patient clinics, and rehabilitation centers. Israel's well-equipped hospitals offer advanced treatments and techniques, including brain surgery, organ transplants, and CAT scans. The country also has a high number of medical professionals for a population of its size, with approximately 27,000 doctors, 44,000 nurses, 8,000 dentists, and 5,000 pharmacists.

▲ U.S. senator Hillary Rodham Clinton practices her first-aid skills on a dummy at the Magen David Adom National Emergency Center in Jerusalem in 2005.

EMERGENCY SERVICES

Israel's medical emergency service is called Magen David Adom. The organization is staffed by 6,000 volunteers, many of whom are secondary school students, who operate from a network of 86 first aid stations around the country. Magen David Adom offers a public ambulance service that includes intensive care units and runs blood banks and a nationwide blood donor program. It also employs 1,200 emergency medical technicians, paramedics, and doctors.

HEALTH PROBLEMS

Israel suffers from the same health problems as many Western nations. About two-thirds of Israelis die from heart disease and cancer. Health education programs have been launched in the country to encourage healthier lifestyles

through diet, exercise, and avoidance of smoking. Health problems in Israel have also been caused by pollution of the country's air and water by heavy industry, intensive farming, and car use.

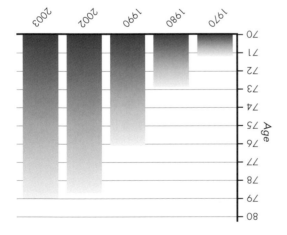

▲ Life expectancy at birth, 1970–2003

CHAPTER 11

Culture and Religion

Modern Israel is a nation of immigrants originating from more than 70 countries. Each community has preserved its own traditions of music, dance, art, and literature. Israeli culture reflects this diversity but has also evolved an identity of its own, often by blending these traditions in unique and innovative ways. The revival and modernization of the ancient language of Hebrew has also been very important in the development of a distinctive Israeli culture.

VISUAL ARTS AND LITERATURE

Israeli artists, sculptors, and photographers have frequently explored issues relating to Jewish history, religion, and identity. Many, such as the painter Reuven Rubin and Yaacov Agam, a

pioneer in optic and kinetic art, have an international reputation. Israeli filmmaking began in the 1950s and has examined subjects such as the Holocaust, the problems faced by immigrants, and the Arab-Israeli conflict.

Most Israeli authors write in Hebrew. They commonly address themes such as the hopes of living in a new state and the Jewish identity. Several have achieved global acclaim, including Amos Oz, Aharon Appelfeld, A.B. Yehoshua, and Shmuel Yosef Agnon. In 1966, Agnon shared the Nobel Prize for Literature. In 2000,

▼ A bookshop in Jerusalem's Old City. Israel's bookstores feature books in many different languages, including Russian, Yiddish, and English.

► Israel's Shiri Maimon (right) performs at the 2005 Eurovision Song Contest. Israel is one of only a few non-European countries to have participated in the contest, with 28 appearances since 1973. It has won the contest three times—in 1978, 1979, and 1998.

Israeli Arab literature received a higher profile in Israel when the Education Ministry included Israeli Arab writers on the curriculum in state secular schools.

PERFORMING ARTS

In classical music, the Israel Philharmonic Orchestra is internationally renowned, as are a number of Israeli classical musicians, including Daniel Barenboim, Itzhak Perlman, and Shlomo Mintz. Israeli popular singers are influenced by both Western and Eastern folk, rock, and pop styles, but their Hebrew lyrics usually reflect uniquely Israeli concerns. The Israeli Arab community likes to perform and listen to Arabic pop music influenced by the music styles of neighboring countries.

Israeli dance is influenced by Jewish folk traditions from Eastern Europe and elsewhere, as well as by classical ballet. Six professional dance companies perform throughout Israel and abroad. Arab and Druze dance troupes often perform traditional dances of North Africa, the Middle East, and southern Asia.

Theater also flourishes in Israel, with a number of professional theaters and dozens of amateur companies performing all over the country. Leading playwrights include Hanoch Levine and Yehoshua Sobol. The national theater is Habimah, in Tel Aviv. There are two Arabic-language theaters that feature original works from Arab countries. One of the few examples of collaboration between the Jewish and Arab communities was a theatrical production of *Romeo and Juliet* in 1994. Performed in a mixture of Hebrew and Arabic, the production received national and international acclaim.

◀ Jews pray at the Western Wall of Solomon's Temple—also known as the Wailing Wall—one of the holiest sites in Judaism.

Nevertheless, Israeli law guarantees freedom of worship for all religions. Each faith community in the country has its own religious council and courts with authority over religious matters and personal issues such as marriage and divorce. The holy sites of each religion are administered by these religious authorities.

JEWS

Among the Jewish community, levels of religious observance vary considerably. About one-fifth of Israel's Jews are Orthodox and observe all the religious laws and practices. About 60 percent of Israeli Jews observe some combination of Jewish laws and principles according to personal choice and ethnic traditions. The remainder are nonobservant.

Many Orthodox Jews play an active role in Israel's national life. Some join religious parties and wield considerable power in the Knesset. Israel also has an ultraorthodox minority (*haredim*) who live an isolated lifestyle in

RELIGION

Religion plays a central part in the lives of many Israelis. The region in which the country was founded has long been a focus for three world religions. It has, consequently, attracted believers from all over the world. Jerusalem, Hebron, Zefat, and Tiberius are the four holy cities of Judaism; Jerusalem, Bethlehem, and Nazareth are holy to Christians; and Jerusalem is sacred to Islam. Haifa is the world center of the Baha'i religion, although there are few Baha'i followers in Israel today.

Because Israel was founded as a Jewish state, the Sabbath (Saturday) and all Jewish festivals and holy days are national holidays.

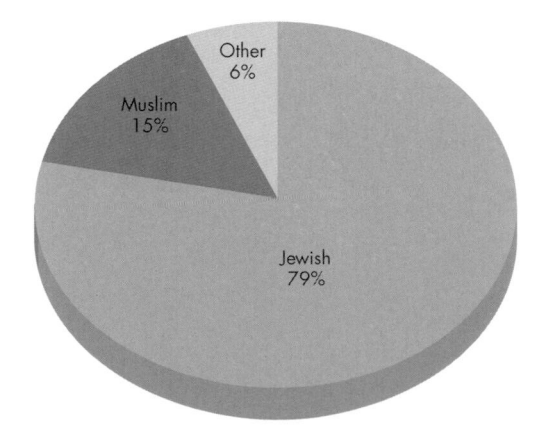

▲ Israel's major religions

separate neighborhoods, dress in traditional clothing, and send their children to their own, privately run schools.

RELIGIOUS MINORITIES

About one million Muslim Arabs live in Israel. Most of them are Sunni Muslims. This includes about 170,000 Bedouin scattered across the south of the country. The Muslim holy sites in Israel are the Haram ash-Sharif building complex on the Temple Mount, which includes the Dome of the Rock and the Al-Aqsa Mosque, in Jerusalem; the Tomb of the Patriarchs, in Hebron; and the El-Jazzar Mosque, in Akko.

Israel also has about 113,000 Christian Arabs, living mainly in towns such as Nazareth, Shfar'am, and Haifa. Most belong to the Greek Catholic, Greek Orthodox, and Roman Catholic churches. The Druze community

consists of about 106,000, living in villages in northern Israel. The Druze religion is similar to Islam, but its beliefs are a secret that is closely guarded by the the community's leaders.

Focus on: Religion and the State

Israel's Jews disagree among themselves on the relationship between religion and the state. Orthodox Jews wish to impose religious law on many aspects of public as well as personal life. Secular Jews see this as threatening Israel's democratic principles. One controversial issue is the definition of a Jew. Orthodox Jews believe a Jew is someone born of a Jewish mother, while secular Jews believe a person can convert to Judaism. Clashes have also occurred over, for example, the observance of the Sabbath as a day of rest. Some Orthodox Jews have been known to stone cars being driven on the Sabbath.

◄ Christian pilgrims take part in the Palm Sunday procession on the Mount of Olives, in Jerusalem's Old City.

CHAPTER 12

Leisure and Tourism

For several decades, Israelis worked six days a week, with Saturday, the Jewish Sabbath, as their day of rest or leisure. In the 1980s, a two-day weekend was introduced, with most businesses (but not schools, banks, or shops) closing on Friday, the Muslim Sabbath.

THE WEEKEND

For Israelis, the weekend begins on Thursday night. In all the big cities, restaurants, cafés, and nightclubs are packed. Tel Aviv, in particular, is known for its energetic nightlife. For non-Muslims, Friday is a day for shopping, cleaning, and other household activities.

For Orthodox Jews, the Sabbath lasts from sunset on Friday to sunset on Saturday. They regard the Sabbath as a day for prayer and

religious study. For secular Jews, Friday night is another popular evening for going out, although many prefer to devote this time to family gatherings at home. For all apart from Orthodox Jews, Saturday is the main day of leisure. Beaches, restaurants, and cafés are filled with people, even though most shops are closed.

GOING OUT

Israelis spend their leisure time in similar ways to citizens of Western nations. They enjoy going to see films and concerts, and they enjoy socializing with friends. Theater is very popular in Israel. Habimah, the national theater, has

▼ Nightlife in Jerusalem. People eat at one of the many cafés and ice cream parlors on Ben Yehuda Street, in the heart of the city's commercial district.

Focus on: Sports in Israel

Favorite sports in Israel include soccer, basketball, gymnastics, swimming, boxing, volleyball, and handball. Of these, the most popular in terms of both participation and viewing are soccer and basketball. Most Israelis prefer to watch soccer on television, with top matches attracting up to 40 percent of the country's viewing audience. Only 30,000 attend live matches featuring teams in the top division each week. In both soccer and basketball, Israel's club and national teams regularly compete in European championships such as Euroleague and Eurobasket (basketball) and the UEFA Champions League (soccer).

Tennis is also popular in Israel. A national network of Israel Tennis Centers has been set up to encourage teenagers to play the sport.

▲ Maccabi Tel Aviv (in yellow) clashes with CSKA Moscow in a European basketball semifinal. Maccabi Tel Aviv is Israel's most successful basketball team and one of the top teams playing in Europe.

The vast majority of Israelis live in towns and cities and enjoy the chance to spend some of their leisure time in the countryside. Kibbutzim and moshavim have responded to this need by building nature parks and theme parks on their lands and offering activities such as horseback riding and kayaking.

With the country's long, hot summers, Israelis like to spend a lot of their free time on the beach. Basketball is a favorite beach sport, as are water skiing and windsurfing. Some wealthy Israelis keep private yachts on marinas along the Mediterranean coast.

over 1,500 seats. It is 90 percent full for most performances, and it has over 30,000 annual subscribers.

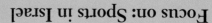

TOURISM

Israel attracts tourists because of its historical, religious, and archaeological sites; its warm climate; and its excellent lakes and beaches. Its peak year for tourism was 2000, with 2.41 million visitors, compared to only 33,000 in 1950. Tourist numbers in Israel typically fall during times of unrest, such as the second intifada and the 2006 conflict between Israel and Hezbollah.

The most popular religious and archaeological sites for tourists in 2004 were the Western Wall, in Jerusalem, visited by 53 percent of tourists; Via Dolorosa, in Jerusalem, visited by 23 percent; and Masada (the scene of a Jewish rebellion against the Romans), near the Dead Sea, visited by 19 percent. Other popular religious destinations are the Dome of the Rock and the Al-Aqsa Mosque, in Jerusalem, and the biblical city of Nazareth. In 2004, 10 percent of Israel's visitors were on a pilgrimage (a journey to a holy place made for religious reasons).

Many people are also attracted by Israel's sunny weather; its geographical diversity; and its modern, well-equipped resorts on the Mediterranean, the Red Sea, the Sea of Galilee,

Tourism in Israel

- Tourist arrivals, millions: 1.063
- Earnings from tourism in U.S.$: 2,379,000,064
- Tourism as % foreign earnings: 5.6%
- Tourist departures, millions: 3.299
- Expenditure on tourism in U.S.$: 3,342,000,128

Source: World Bank

and the Dead Sea. Most of Israel's tourists are from Europe and North America. In 2004, 37 percent arrived from Western Europe and 28 percent came from North America. Tourism is very important to Israel's economy. About 40,000 Israelis work in the tourist industry. In 2003, tourists brought in almost U.S.$2.4 billion.

TRAVELING ISRAELIS

Israelis are frequent travelers, with nearly 3.3 million traveling abroad in 2003 on vacation or business. Western Europe and North America are popular destinations for Israeli tourists, as is Egypt, especially the Sinai Peninsula. Since the 1994 peace treaty with Jordan, many Israelis have vacationed there, visiting sites such as

▶ Pilgrims and tourists gather at the Church of the Nativity, located in Bethlehem in the West Bank. It is one of the oldest churches in the world, and it is regarded as the birthplace of Jesus Christ.

Petra. The fall of the communist regimes in Eastern Europe in 1989 prompted many Israelis to explore their roots in places such as Prague, Budapest, and Warsaw. Cheap package holidays to Turkey and Greece have become popular, and many young Israelis backpack to places such as India, China, and Latin America.

Resorts in Israel are also popular destinations for Israelis, especially those located in Galilee; by the Dead Sea; and in Elat, on the Red Sea. In 2004, Israelis accounted for 91 percent of visitors to Elat and 88 percent of visitors to the Dead Sea and Galilee.

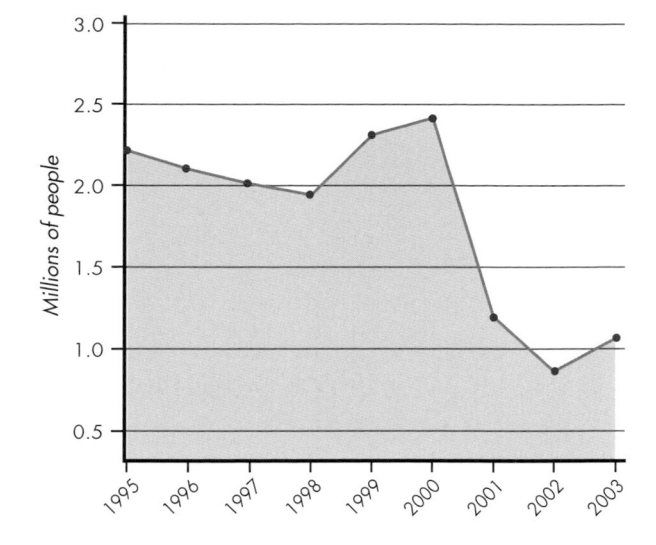

▲ Changes in international tourism, 1995–2003

Focus on: Israel's Museums

Israel has about 150 museums, which receive about 10 million visitors each year. The Israel Museum, which opened in Jerusalem in 1965, contains the Dead Sea Scrolls, a series of ancient Hebrew and Aramaic manuscripts. It also houses collections of Jewish art and sculpture and archaeological finds from the region. The Yad Vashem Museum in Jerusalem—a powerful memorial to the 6 million Jews who died in the Holocaust—is one of Israel's most-visited museums. In Tel Aviv, the Diaspora Museum explores the history of the Jewish people. The country also has collections of ancient and modern art in museums in Tel Aviv and Haifa. The L.A. Mayer Institute for Islamic Art, located in Jerusalem, displays Arabic and Islamic art and sculpture.

◀ This Red Sea resort in Elat attracts tourists with its colorful fish and corals, red mountains, sandy beaches, and clear blue waters.

CHAPTER 13

Environment and Conservation

I n its short history, Israel has undergone large-scale industrial and agricultural expansion in order to meet the demands of its rapidly growing population. Today, most of its citizens enjoy Western standards of living. The country's high rate of car use and people's attachment to a wide range of consumer goods have had a damaging effect on Israel's environment.

WATER POLLUTION

Many of Israel's 40 major rivers have been contaminated by agricultural or industrial waste or sewage from nearby towns and cities. For example, the Kishon River that flows through Haifa has been severely polluted by raw industrial waste from nearby chemical factories. To combat this problem, the Ministry of the Environment has established 16 river restoration projects and improved sewage treatment plants to prevent the discharge of

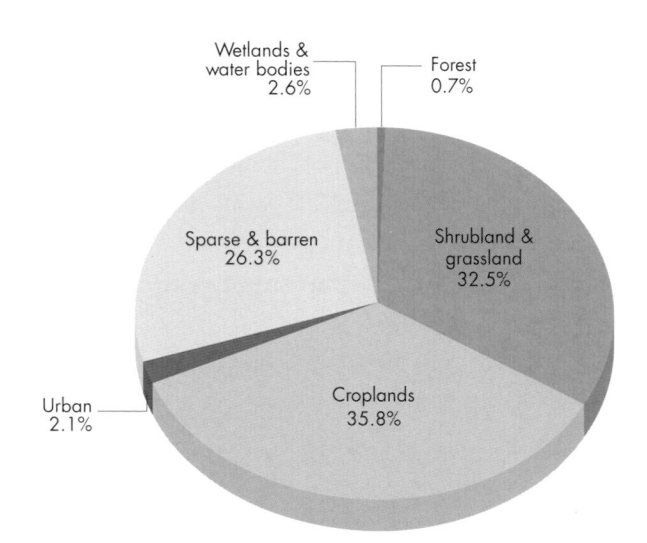

▲ Types of habitat

sewage into rivers. River polluters have been given tough punishment. Among the rivers being restored are the Lachish, Zippori, Yarkon, and Kishon, on the Mediterranean coast; and the Harod and Southern Jordan, in eastern Israel. Recreation and tourist sites have been established on some of Israel's rivers, including the Kishon, Taninim, and Hadera.

Israel also faces pollution of its Mediterranean and Red Sea coastlines from oil and chemical spills, industrial pollution, and the dumping of waste and litter in the sea or on beaches. The

◀ This stork is one of 200 that were poisoned by wastewater from a chemical plant near the town of Dimona, in the Negev. Israel is a stopping-off point for thousands of storks on their annual migration from Europe to Africa.

◀ These busy intersecting highways are near the town of Lakhish. The rising number of cars on Israel's roads is a major reason for the increase in air pollution in the country.

Mediterranean is particularly affected because 70 percent of the country's population is concentrated here. Israel's government has taken steps to protect this environment by, for example, limiting development of coastal industry and resorts.

AIR POLLUTION

Vehicle use, electricity production, and industry all contribute to Israel's poor air quality, particularly on the heavily developed Mediterranean coastal plain. Between 1995 and 2005, the number of vehicles in Israel nearly doubled, as did the country's electricity consumption. Air quality analyses show high levels of a range of pollutants, including suspended particulate matter, sulphur dioxide, nitrogen oxides, and carbon dioxide. In 2005, Israel's government set up an air-quality management system to monitor air pollution levels throughout the country. It can warn vulnerable citizens to stay indoors on high-pollution days. The government has attempted to improve air quality by encouraging car users to use public transportation, introducing improvements in vehicle fuel quality, and getting industries to agree to lower their emissions of pollutants. In July 2004, the Israel Electric Corporation switched to very low sulphur fuel in its oil-burning power plants.

Focus on: Waste and Recycling

Because of population growth and rising living standards, Israel's solid waste output (both domestic and industrial) has been growing by about 5 percent per year. In 2003, the whole country produced about 5.5 million tons (5 million metric tons) of solid waste. In tackling this problem, Israel's government has focused on sustainable solutions, such as waste reduction, recycling (including composting), reuse, and energy recovery. Israel currently recycles about 20 percent of its garbage. Its government has set a recycling rate target of 50 percent by 2010.

CONSERVATION

Israel has a rich variety of plants and animals, including about 2,317 plant species (150 of which are unique to Israel). In a small, highly industrialized and urbanized country, this diversity is constantly under threat. Today, many of Israel's animal species are endangered, including the leopard, fire salamander, green turtle, and lesser kestrel.

Focus on: Reintroducing Biblical Wildlife

Since 1969, the Israel Nature and National Parks Protection Authority (INNPPA) has been carrying out a long-term project to reintroduce animals mentioned in the Bible to the land of Israel. According to the Bible, lions, leopards, bears, and cheetahs all once roamed the landscape. Today, only a few leopards remain in Israel. Hippopotamuses, crocodiles, deer, oryx, and onager, which are also referred to in the Bible, had all disappeared from Israel by the 1960s. INNPPA set up two protected breeding facilities, called Hai Bar (Hebrew for *wildlife*) Reserves, where the species to be reintroduced could be bred. The process of reintroducing them is very slow, but INNPPA hopes that these species eventually will be able to thrive, as their ancestors once did, in the wild. So far, five species have been successfully reintroduced.

▲ A pair of Arabian oryx graze in one of the Hai Bar Reserves in which Biblical wildlife are bred.

Israel currently has about 184 nature reserves and national parks that cover about 19 percent of its land area. Most of these protected areas are situated in the country's sparsely populated desert regions. Only about 3 percent of the Mediterranean coastal plain is protected. Outside these protected areas, Israel's biodiversity is threatened by various factors. These include the construction and development of towns and cities; the breaking up of habitats through road- and fence-building, which blocks the exchange of plants and animals; the introduction of non-native species, which upsets the ecological balance; unregulated hunting and fishing; and environmental pollution.

Israel's Mediterranean coastline is one of the country's most threatened ecosystems. The building of tourist resorts and unregulated mining have led to the loss of over two-thirds of its Mediterranean coastal sand areas and the extinction and decline of many species, including the sea turtle. Overexploitation of water resources and the reclamation of swamps have destroyed many of Israel's wetland areas and also caused the extinction of many species. To address these problems, the country's government set up the National Biodiversity Strategy and Action Plan in 2003. As part of this plan, the government aims to organize public-awareness campaigns, conduct research, pass legislation, and introduce incentives for the protection and conservation of the country's wildlife. In addition, 220 more nature reserves and 50 more national parks are planned.

Environmental and Conservation Data

- Forested area as % total land area: 0.7%
- Protected area as % total land area: 19.1%
- Number of protected areas: 184

SPECIES DIVERSITY

Category	Known species	Threatened species
Mammals	116	14
Breeding birds	162	12
Reptiles	99	4
Amphibians	8	n/a
Fish	178	1
Plants	2,317	n/a

Source: World Resources Institute

► The Jerusalem Botanical Gardens, which opened to the public in 1985, contains more than 6,000 plant species. These species were brought to Israel from all over the world.

CHAPTER 14

Future Challenges

▲ These Jewish settlers were forced to leave their homes in settlements on the Gaza Strip during the Israeli pull-out from the territory in August 2005. Though painful for the settlers, Israel's government saw this pull-out as a necessary step on the road to lasting peace settlement with the Palestinians.

I n its short history, Israel has overcome serious threats to its survival, fighting and winning five wars against its Arab neighbors. Today, various armed organizations and terrorist networks continue to threaten Israel, and conflict in the region remains unresolved. Other challenges facing Israel include continued population growth and scarcity of resources. It also faces challenges to its very identity as a Jewish state.

WATER SCARCITY

Water scarcity is a critical challenge for Israel. Pioneering efforts in water efficiency will need to continue to meet the country's needs. Greater recycling of wastewater for irrigation, preventing the pollution of natural waterways, and the encouragement of water conservation among the population are all key strategies for

the future. Water is especially important as it is a major source of tension in the Middle East. Israel shares its main water resources with Syria and Jordan and is dependent on political agreements over water use with these countries. Future scarcity could strain these agreements and ultimately lead to conflict.

POPULATION GROWTH

Israel's population is eight times larger than it was in 1948, largely because of immigration. Immigration has benefited Israel's economy and given it a rich and diverse culture, but it has also brought challenges. Integrating so many different cultures has not always been easy. Some of Israel's immigrant communities have found it hard to adapt to Israel's Western-style society. Economically, the country has a growing gap between rich and poor. Population growth also places greater pressure on the country's resources and environment.

RESOLVING THE CONFLICT

Reaching a lasting peace with the Palestinians and neighboring Arab states is Israel's most significant challenge. It will require controversial issues to be resolved, such as the status of Jerusalem and the West Bank, and the establishment of a recognized Palestinian state. Israel has made bold moves toward peace, but it has also suffered setbacks. On July 12, 2006, Hezbollah fighters in southern Lebanon seized two Israeli soldiers and launched rocket attacks on Israeli settlements. Israel responded with an air and ground offensive that escalated into 34 days of conflict between Israel and Hezbollah. About 1,400 people died (many of them civilians) and 1.5 million were forced to flee their homes. A United Nations ceasefire ended the fighting, but the rift between Israel and its enemies appears as wide as ever. Ultimately, the political process must succeed for peace between Israel and its opponents in the Middle East to last.

▲ Israeli and Palestinian musicians perform together in the West Bank city of Ramallah in August 2005. Collaborations such as this help to foster links between the two communities.

Time Line

1890s Zionist movement begins.

1897 Founding of the World Zionist Organization.

1900s Clashes between Palestinians and Jewish settlers begin.

1918 Fall of the Ottoman Empire.

1920 Histadrut (General Federation of Labor) is founded.

1920–1948 British Mandate of Palestine.

1929 Founding of the Jewish Agency for Israel.

1932 The first Maccabiah Games are held.

1947 (November) UN General Assembly accepts plan to partition Palestine into two countries. **(December)** Fighting between Palestinian Arabs and Jews begins.

1948 (April) Jewish terrorists massacre about 120 Palestinian Arab civilians at the village of Deir Yassin, near Jerusalem. **(May)** Israel declares independence. Neighboring Arab states invade.

1948–1949 726,000 Palestinian Arabs become refugees.

1949 Armistice agreements between Israel and the invading Arab states end the war. Israel joins the United Nations.

1950 Knesset passes the Law of Return, allowing any Jew to settle in Israel.

1952 Israel Atomic Energy Commission is set up.

1956 (July-October) Egyptian leader Nasser closes the Suez Canal to Israeli shipping and blockades the Straits of Tiran. Israel invades Gaza Strip and Sinai Peninsula.

1957 (March) Israel withdraws from Sinai and Gaza.

1958 MASHAV (Center for International Cooperation) is founded.

1963–1964 Israel builds its National Water Carrier.

1964 Formation of the PLO.

1967 (June) Six-Day War: Israel carries out a preemptive strike on Egypt, Jordan, and Syria, capturing the Gaza Strip and the Sinai Peninsula, the Golan Heights, and the West Bank. **(November)** UN Security Council Resolution 242 calls on Israel to withdraw from seized territories and all states in the area to respect each others' independence.

1973 (October) Yom Kippur War: Egypt and Syria launch a joint invasion of Israel. Israel pushes back the invaders but suffers heavy losses.

1974–1975 Israel withdraws most of its forces from Sinai.

1978 (September) Israel and Egypt negotiate a peace agreement at Camp David.

1979 (March) Israel and Egypt sign a peace treaty.

1981 Israel formally annexes East Jerusalem and the Golan Heights.

1982 (June-August) Israel invades Lebanon and lays siege to Beirut, forcing the PLO to leave Lebanon.

1984 Israel's inflation rate reaches 445 percent.

1985 (June) Israel's forces partially withdraw from Lebanon, maintaining a security zone 5 miles (8 km) wide along the border.

1987–1993 First intifada.

1990s Almost one million Jews from the former Soviet Union emigrate to Israel.

1991 Middle East peace process begins with a conference in Madrid.

1993 (September) Oslo Accords between Israel and the PLO are signed in Washington, D.C.

1994 Israel signs a peace treaty with Jordan.

1994–1999 Israeli forces begin to withdraw from the West Bank, but the peace process stalls.

1996 Israel launches AMOS, its first satellite.

2000 (May) Israel completes its withdrawal from Lebanon. **(July)** Israeli and PLO leadership attempt to restart the peace process at Camp David, but talks end in deadlock. **(September)** Second intifada begins.

2002 (April-June) Israeli forces invade and reoccupy seven West Bank towns in order to destroy terrorist infrastructure. **(June)** Israel begins construction of a security fence around the Palestinian-controlled areas of the West Bank.

2003 (April) Launch of the "road map to peace," a UN-backed plan to bring peace to the Middle East.

2005 (August) In a unilateral gesture of peace, Israel dismantles the Jewish settlements in the Gaza Strip and hands the territory over to the Palestinian Authority.

2006 (January) Prime Minister Ariel Sharon suffers a massive stroke. Radical Islamic group Hamas becomes the majority party in the Palestinian Legislative Council. **(March)** Kadima, a new party founded by Ariel Sharon, wins the most seats in the Knesset election and pledges to continue to disengage from the occupied territories and fix the final borders of Israel. **(April)** Ehud Olmert becomes prime minister. **(June)** Israel launches air strikes on Gaza in response to the abduction of an Israeli soldier by Hamas militants. **(July)** Israel launches a ground and air offensive in southern Lebanon in response to the abduction of Israeli soldiers by Hezbollah fighters. **(August)** UN ceasefire put into effect for the purpose of halting fighting between Israel and Hezbollah.

Glossary

anti-Semitic having to to with hatred of Jews

aqueduct a pipe or channel for moving water to a lower level, often across a great distance

Baha'i a religion founded in Iran in 1863 that teaches that all religions have value, that humankind is spiritually one, and which advocates world peace

Bedouin a nomadic Arab people who live in the desert areas of North Africa and the Middle East

biodiversity the range of organisms that exist in an ecosystem

capitalist having to do with an economic system in which trade and industry are controlled by private owners for profit

communist having to do with a government in which the state controls wealth, property, trade, and the means of production, such as that of the Soviet Union between 1918 and 1990

constituency one of the areas into which a country is divided for election purposes

constitution a written document outlining the basic laws or principles by which a country is governed

desertification the process by which fertile land is degraded into barren desert

Diaspora the dispersal of the Jews from Palestine following the destruction by the Romans of the Second Temple in A.D. 70

Druze a people who follow a religion similar to Islam who are found mainly in Israel, Lebanon, and Syria

ecosystem a group of interdependent organisms together with the environment they inhabit and depend upon

Gross Domestic Product (GDP) the total value of all goods and services produced within a country in a year minus income from investments in other countries

Hamas a Palestinian Islamic fundamentalist group known for terrorist attacks on Isreal

Hebrew the ancient Semitic language that is today spoken in a modernized form by the people of Israel

Hezbollah a radical Islamic group based in Lebanon that is supported by Iran and known for terrorist attacks on Israel

intifada Arabic for "shaking off"; the Palestinian uprising in the occupied territories that took place between 1987 and 1993 and the second Palestinian uprising that began in September 2000

liberal-democratic state a state with a political system that has free elections, a number of political parties, and political decisions made through an independent legislature and judiciary

nationalist having to do with devotion to a nation and views in which that nation is placed above all others

occupied territories those territories seized by Israel in the 1967 Six-Day War, including the West Bank and (until August 2005) the Gaza Strip

oil shale a black or dark brown type of sedimentary rock from which petroleum can be extracted

Orthodox following the traditional rules of a faith

Palestine Liberation Organization (PLO) an organization of Palestinian Arabs dedicated to the establishment of an independent Palestinian state in the West Bank, Gaza, and possibly part or all of Israel

Palestinian Authority (PA) a Palestinian-run governing body with limited power over the Palestinian territory in the West Bank and full power over the Gaza Strip

privatize to transfer to private ownership a business or public utility that has been under state ownership

refugee a person who seeks or takes shelter, often from war or persecution, by going to a foreign country

Sabbath a day of rest and religious worship

secular not religious

socialist having to do with or believing in a political system in which wealth is shared equally between people and main industries and trade are controlled by the government

Sunni the largest branch of Islam, which believes in the traditions of the Sunna and accepts the first four caliphs as rightful successors to Muhammad

trade union an organization established to help and protect the rights of workers in an industry

vocational training training for a particular job

welfare state a political system in which the government takes primary responsibility for assuring the basic health and welfare of its citizens

Zionism the worldwide movement that worked to establish a Jewish nation in Palestine and has given support to Israel since its founding in 1948

Further Information

BOOKS TO READ

Bowden, Rob. *Jerusalem*
(Great Cities of the the World).
World Almanac Library, 2006.

Finkelstein, Norman. *Ariel Sharon* (A & E Biography).
Lerner Publications, 2005.

Fisher, Fredrick. *Israel*
(Countries of the World).
Gareth Stevens, 2000.

Keene, Michael. *Judaism*
(Religions of the World).
World Almanac Library, 2006.

Marguiles, Philip. *The Creation of Israel*
(Turning Points in World History).
Greenhaven Press, 2005.

Rackers, Mark (editor). *The Arab-Israeli Conflict* (Great Speeches in History).
Greenhaven Press, 2004.

Uschan, Michael V. *Suicide Bombings in Israel and Palestinian Terrorism*
(Terrorism in Today's World). World Almanac Library, 2006.

Various authors. World Almanac Library of the Middle East. World Almanac Library, 2006.

Woolf, Alex. *The Arab-Israeli Conflict* (Atlas of Conflicts) World Almanac Library, 2005.

USEFUL WEB SITES

CIA World Factbook: Israel
www.cia.gov/cia/publications/factbook/geos/is.html

Israel Ministry of Foreign Affairs
www.mfa.gov.il/mfa/

The New York Times-Israel News
topics.nytimes.com/top/news/international/countriesandterritories/israel/index.html

Shattered Dreams of Peace: The Road from Oslo
www.pbs.org/wgbh/pages/frontline/shows/oslo/

World Almanac for Kids Online: Israel
www.worldalmanacforkids.com/explore/nations/israel.html

World Health Organization: Israel
www.who.int/countries/isr/en/

Index

Page numbers in **bold** indicate pictures.

agriculture 14, 20, 26, **27**, 28–29, **28**, **29**, 33, 37, 42, 45, 54
air pollution 45, 55
air travel 39, **39**
Al-Aqsa Mosque 6, **6**, 49, 52
AMOS satellite 40
anti-Semitism 9, 34
Arab population 19, **25**, 32, 33, 42, 47
Arabic (language) 19, 42, 47
Arab-Israeli conflicts 4, 5, 10, 36, 46, 58
Arafat, Yasser **12**
art 43, 46, 53
Ashdod 40
Ashkenazic Jews 18, 19, 24, 33

Baha'i 48
Balfour Declaration 9
Bedouin 19, 49
Beersheba 21, 39
Ben-Gurion, David **10**
Bethlehem 48, 52, **52**
Bible 4, 6
British Mandate 9, 10, 36

cars 38, 45, 49, 54, 55, **55**
Christianity/Christians 6, 19, 21, 48, 49, **49**, **52**
climate 16–17, 52
cloud seeding 27, 29
coal 26
communications 6, 31, 40–41
conservation 56–57

dance 46, 47
Dead Sea 15, **15**, 16, 26, 28, 52, 53
Dead Sea Scrolls 53
desalination 27–28, 29
diamonds 31, **31**, 32
Diaspora 8
Diaspora Museum 53
Dome of the Rock **6**, **21**, 49, 52
Druze 19, **19**, 42, 47, 49

East Jerusalem 11, **13**, 14, 21
economy 30–33, 52
education 23, 25, 31, 33, 42–43
Egged 39
Egypt 10, 11, 12, 26, 36, 52
El Al 39, **39**
Elat 17, 28, 39, 40, 53, **53**
elections 25, **25**
electricity 26, 55
exports 28, 29, 32

Falashas **34**
fishing 29, 57

Galilee 20, 28, 53
Gaza Strip 10, 11, 12, 13, **58**
Golan Heights 6, 17, 11, 14
government 22–25, 33

Hai Bar Reserves 56, **56**
Haifa 14, 16, 20, 21, **32**, 39, 40, 48, 49, 53, 54
Hamas 13
health care 6, 25, 37, 44–45, **44**, **45**
Hebrew (language) 19, 42, 43, 46, 47
Hebrews 8
Hebron 48
Histadrut 33
Holocaust 9, **9**, 46, 53

immigration 5, 9, 18, 20, 30, 31, 37, **37**, 46, 59
imports 26, 32
industry 14, 21, 27, 29, **30**, 31, **31**, 32, 33, 45, 54
Internet 41, **41**
intifada **4**, 12, 13, 33, 34, 52
irrigation 27, **27**, 28, **28**, 29, 58
Islam/Muslims 4, 6, 8, 19, 21, **21**, 48, 49

Jerusalem **6**, 8, 16, **17**, 20, **20**, 21, **21**, **22**, **23**, 39, **40**, **41**, **46**, 48, **48**, **49**, **50**, 52, 53, **57**, 59
Jewish Agency for Israel 37
Jewish festivals 48
Jewish population 4, 9, 18–19
Jewish state 4, 5, 9, 10, 11, 37, 48, 58
Jordan (Transjordan) 10, 11, 15, 36, 52–53, 58
Jordan River 6, 10, 16, **16**, 25, 27, 58
Judah 4, 8
Judaism 6, 21, 48
justice system 23

Kadima 24
Khamsin 16
kibbutzim 29, 51
Kishon, River 16, 54
Knesset 18, 22–23, **22**, **23**, 24, 25, 48

Labor 24
Lebanon 10, 12
leisure 21, 50–51
Likud 24
literature 46–47
local government 23

Maccabiah Games 36, **36**
Magen David Adom 45, **45**
manufacturing 32

Masada **8**, 52
MASHAV (Center for International Cooperation) 36–37
media 33, 40
Mediterranean coast 4, 14, 16, 20, 21, 29, 51, 54–55, 57, 59
military service 43
minerals 15, 26, 28
moshavim 29, 51
music 5, 43, 46, 47, **47**, **59**

national parks 56, **56**, 57
National Water Carrier 27
Nazareth 6, 48, 49, 52
Negev Desert 14, **14**, 15, 17, 20, 21, 26, **26**, **27**, 28, **28**, **38**, **54**
newspapers 40
nuclear power 26

occupied territories 11, 12, 24, 33, 34
oil 26
Olmert, Ehud 24, **24**
Orthodox Jews **20**, 42, **43**, 48–49, 50
Oslo Accords 12-13, **12**, 25

Palestine 8, 9, 10, 20
Palestine Liberation Organization (PLO) 11, 12
Palestinian Authority (PA) 13, 25
Palestinian population 4, 5, 9, 18, 19, 21, 33, 59
peace negotiations 12, 13, 25, 34, **35**
political parties 24
pollution 45, 54–55, 58
population growth 18, 58, 59
ports 20, 21, **32**, 40
poverty 33, **33**, 59
prime minister **12**, 22, 23, **35**
public transport 38–39, 55
publishing 47

Rabin, Yitzhak **12**
railways 38–39
recycling 55, 58
Red Sea 16, 29, 52, **53**, 54
refugees 10
religion 18, **21**, 23, 24, 48–49, **48**, **49**, **52**
religious courts 23
Rift Valley 14, 15, 16, **16**
"road map to peace" 13
roads 38, **38**
Russia/Russians 5, 9, 19

schools 19, 42, **42**, 43, **43**
Sea of Galilee (Lake Kinneret) **5**, 15, 16, 27, 52, 58
security fence 13, **13**, 34
Sephardic Jews 18, **18**, 19, 24, 33
service industries 29, 31, 32
Sharon, Ariel 24, **35**
Sinai Peninsula 11, **11**, 12, 52
Six-Day War 11, **11**, 21, 34
solar energy 26, **26**
sport 51, **51**
Suez War 11
Syria 10, 11, 12, 15, 58

Tel Aviv **10**, 20, 26, **33**, 39, 50, 53
Tel Aviv-Yafo 16, 20, 21
telephones **40**, 41
television 40, 43
terrorism 10, 11, 13, 44
theater 47, 50–51
Tiberius 48
tourism 29, 31, 52–53, **53**, 57
trade deficit 31, 32
transport 6, 31, 38–40

United Nations 4, 10, 11, 13, 21, 34–35, **35**
universities 43

Via Dolorosa 6, 52

waste 55
water 15, 26, 27, 45, 58
West Bank **4**, 10, 11, 12, 13, 14, 25, 59, **59**
Western Wall **6**, 48, 52
wildlife 56–57, **54**, **56**
World Zionist Organization 37

Yad Vashem Museum **9**, 53
Yafo 20
Yarkon, River 16, 54
Yiddish 19
Yom Kippur 12
Yom Kippur War 12

Zefat 48
Zionism 9, 35, 58

About the Author

Alex Woolf studied History and Government at Essex University. He has written more than 20 children's books on history, geography, and social issues, including *Atlas of Conflicts: The Arab-Israeli Conflict*. He lives with his wife and son in Southgate, North London.